The Anatomy of a 7 Figure Medical Practice - The Ultimate System For Doctors To Building A Practice With More Profits and Less Hassle

ISBN: 978-0-578-82055-2

(704) 626 1298

www.SRPMedicalMarketing.com

www.CallWithMatt.com

Disclaimer

The material in this publication is of the nature of general comment only, and does not represent professional advice. It is not intended to provide specific guidance for particular circumstances and it should not be relied on as the basis for any decision to take action or not take action on any matter which it covers.

Readers should obtain professional advice where appropriate, before making any such decision.

To the maximum extent permitted by law, the author and publisher disclaim all responsibility and liability to any person, arising directly or indirectly from any person taking or not taking action based on the information in this publication.

The Anatomy of a 7 Figure Medical Practice

The Ultimate System For Doctors To Building A Practice With More Profits and Less Hassle

Matthew J Gillogly

Table of Contents

CHAPTER 1

A Tale of Two Doctors

I'd like to tell you the story of two doctors who went to the same medical school, had the same grades and the same opportunities when they graduated.

Yet, they ended up in two very different positions over the next 20 years.

Both doctors did everything by the book. Upon graduation, they entered the world full of promise for young professionals in their position.

Each doctor wanted to have their own practice. They were extremely excited about the opportunity to help people and change their lives for the better. Both doctors wanted to treat their patients well and be experts in their field. Patients and colleagues would respect them, and they'd follow their passion and do their best work.

But at the same time, both doctors wanted a life of success, not just in the professional sense. Rather, they strived toward the financial achievements that their professions carried.

The first goal of the doctors in question was to get out of the massive college debt. They each paid $250,000 for the opportunity to chase after their dreams and live a fulfilling life. And now it was time to repay for that opportunity.

Upon doing so, the doctors would be able to keep on living a successful and fulfilling life.

Sadly, one doctor never achieved this. Despite starting in the same strong position as his colleague, his road was anything but successful.

Upon graduating, he tried starting his own practice. But he couldn't find a way to grow it. He'd work crazy hours every day, trying to get his practice off the ground.

However, any success he'd achieve would be short-lived.

As a result, the doctor was still buried in debt for years after graduating. Eventually, he gave up on his practice altogether. There was just no way for it to keep growing. Because of this, the doctor threw in the towel and went on to work for a massive hospital group, where every patient was just a number.

Dissatisfied with his career, the doctor would switch jobs every 18–24 months. He'd go from one hospital to another, but they were all the same.

The doctor started a few side hustles, hoping that they'd enrich the life that he'd worked so hard for. But unfortunately, none of his ventures managed to get off the ground.

The worst part was, all these struggles didn't only impact the doctor on a professional level. His family life started suffering as well, which resulted in him separating from his wife.

So, after all those years of hard work, the doctor ended up in a place where no professional wants to find themselves. He was all alone, jumping from one clinic to the other. He drove a beat-up Ford, which he couldn't even afford to fix. Despite all his efforts to find a way out, it seemed like there was none.

The second doctor, on the other hand, achieved everything he'd dreamt of, and then some.

He opened his practice, which gradually became well-known in the market. Patients would keep coming, and they'd receive the treatment they needed. Patients had fantastic experiences with the doctor, and they saw him as a trusted and reliable solution to their issues.

The consequence of this was astonishing success. The doctor was able to create the life he'd always dreamed of. Paying off that huge college debt wasn't an issue, as the financial rewards followed his great professional achievements.

In fact, the reward got big enough to allow the doctor to create his ideal lifestyle. He could run his practice without struggles while still having enough time to enjoy his life. He could devote himself to his family, pursue his other passions, and live an overall exciting life.

So how did this happen?

How come two people with the exact same predispositions went in completely opposite directions?

Was it luck? Was the second doctor in the right place at the right time?

Not exactly…

The Two Skill Sets

The purpose of this book is to show you why one doctor succeeded while the other didn't. Of course, the ultimate goal is to show you what you have to do if you want to live the life of the successful doctor.

And in essence, it all comes down to developing the right kind of skills.

You see, most doctors assume that medical skills are enough to build a thriving practice. But this is the exact mistake that the first doctor made, and that cost him a lot.

There's no doubt that medical skills are critical. But they're only one part of the equation. The other one is business skills.

Unfortunately, the first doctor didn't understand this. He thought that developing his medical skills further would help him succeed. But that never happened.

The second doctor, on the other hand, knew that he should look at his practice as a business venture. On top of helping patients, he understood that the practice should be a full-fledged business.

This is why he sought help and developed the necessary skills. He got the right business and marketing training, which allowed him to position his practice uniquely in the market. This allowed the doctor to draw in more and more patients, which resulted in explosive growth.

So, if you want to live a life full of passion, this is what you need to do. You must add this business dimension to your practice if you want to make it. And this book will show you how to do it.

But first, let me discuss the true reason why many doctors can't find a way to grow.

Why Do Doctors Struggle in Their Own Practices?

Right now, you might feel stuck in your practice. You know that there's more to it than you're currently achieving. You're confident in your ability to truly change people's lives for the better.

And yet, nothing you do seems to let you explore your full potential.

If this is how you feel, know that you're not the only one. In fact, many doctors are going through the same experience.

But why?

Let me introduce the concept I call the cash-based practice paradox. Once you understand it, you'll uncover the key reason behind all your struggles.

As I explained, growing a practice requires two types of skills – business and medical.

The business skill set is on the vertical line, and the medical skill set is on the horizontal line. These two skill sets create four quadrants, with each doctor falling into one of them.

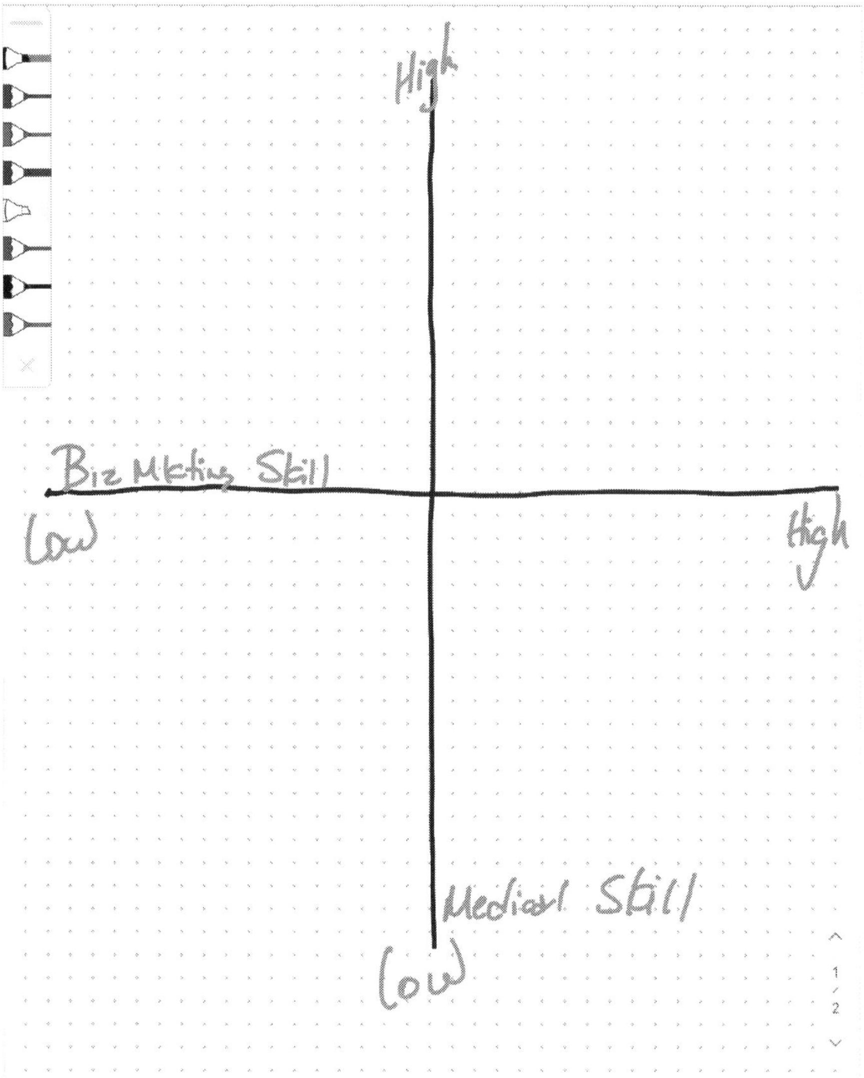

If your medical and business skills are low, you'll be in the danger zone. Starting and running a high-performing practice will be a perpetual struggle.

Luckily, very few doctors are in this category, as medical school alone provides more than adequate training. Upon graduation, you'll likely have highly developed medical skills. And this will make you go up the medical skill axis.

But if your business skills stay low, you'll still struggle. This is what I call the caution zone. And it's the exact place where the second doctor from the story found himself. Even though he kept working on his medical skills, it wouldn't bring him any closer to success. He just continued to move in this one direction without focusing on his business skills.

Now, you'll be in the same zone if it's the other way around – high business skills paired with low medical skills. In my opinion, this is the worst kind of doctor. They can sell just about anything, but they can't actually help their patients.

The quadrant you want to find yourself in is the fourth one – high medical *and* business skills. Ultimately, these are the doctors that achieve the biggest things and the greatest financial security for their family.

The successful doctor from the story you read is in this quadrant. The main reason why he succeeded is that he took the time to build the right business skills.

After graduating, he realized that he needed to match this skill set with medical expertise. And this powerful combination allowed him to create the life that he'd envisioned.

But the reality is, many doctors don't understand this. If you find yourself struggling, you might think that it's due to a lack of talent or knowledge. And this will make you fall down the rabbit hole of constantly honing your medical skills to perfection.

At the same time, you won't work on your business acumen. And *that's* the true reason why your practice will struggle to grow.

The thing is, you don't need to be the absolute best in your field to succeed. I've met many extremely capable and knowledgeable doctors who struggled to grow despite their expertise.

There's a high chance that you've already checked this box. You've likely built up your medical skills enough to make a lasting positive change in people's lives.

Now, it's time to focus on your business prowess. And yes, you *can* master all the skills you need. In fact, you can do it much more easily than you might think. It's nowhere as daunting as doctors usually assume.

But before you start working on your skills, you must learn what a successful practice looks like from a business perspective. So, let me give you a quick overview which I'll then expand on further in the book.

The Three Components to Running a Cash-Based Practice

So, we've established that you'll want to create a cash-based practice if you want to succeed. But what does that look like in action?

The thing is, there are quite some moving parts to making this happen. But it all comes down to the three critical components that you need to have in place.

Think of them as the foundation of your practice. If you set it up nicely from the get-go, everything else will fall into place more smoothly.

The first component that you need to focus on is steady patient flow. After all, this is what makes your practice viable in the long run. If you have these huge peaks and valleys when it comes to your patients, you can't have a reliable cash flow. You'll have spikes followed by dry spells, and you won't know what to expect from your practice.

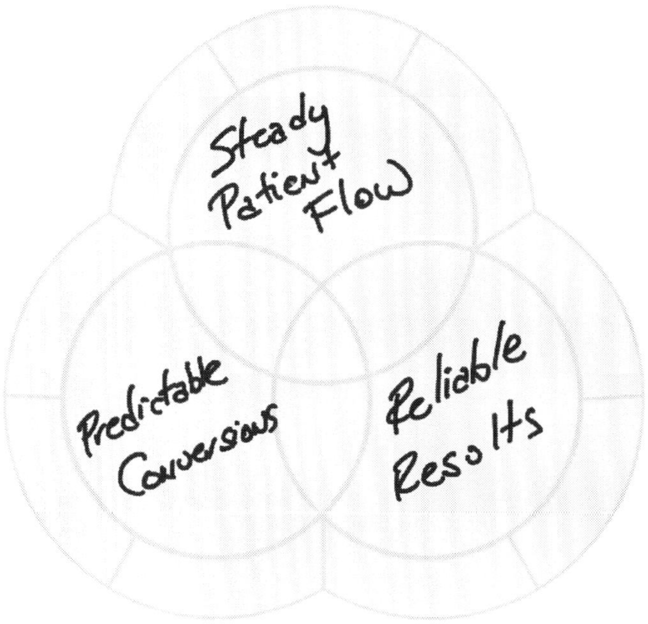

That's why a steady patient flow is the foundation of success. But it's still not enough to create a lifestyle that you want to build for yourself.

That's why the second component that you'll want to add is predictable conversions. And this is where things start coming together. You start getting the thing that I'm sure you want more of – money.

But does this mean that you're now achieving all your goals?

Well, not exactly.

You see, there's one more component that every cash-based practice needs – reliable results for patients.

A steady patient flow with reliable results will give you more time, which is what most doctors need. And when you combine predictable conversions with reliable results, you can start scaling your practice.

When you can scale your practice, you can rest assured that it will keep growing in a leveraged way. So, you don't only have a steady patient flow with good results. On top of this, you have a way to ensure that your practice keeps growing uninterruptedly.

And when you have all three of these things in place, you get the final aspect of a fulfilling life that's at the center of it all:

Freedom.

At the end of the day, this is what you want to fill your lifestyle with – money, time, and freedom. This is how you truly succeed and know that all your efforts have been worth it.

Now, these three components need to work together if you want to create a cash-based practice. And in this book, you'll see how to make it happen.

Live the Lifestyle You Deserve

You didn't go to medical school and overcome all those challenges to turn your life into a struggle. The value you provide as a doctor is far too great for you to make compromises. You deserve to run a practice that lets you achieve all your lifestyle goals.

Right now, you have a pretty good idea of what this looks like. Remember that it all comes down to developing the skills that doctors overlook. Instead of just being a practice owner, you must also be a business owner if you want to succeed.

Once you understand this, you can build a cash-based practice. And when you build all three of the mentioned components into it, you'll see what your practice is truly capable of.

Of course, I'm not just here to tell you what to do, but *how* to do it as well. Throughout this book, you'll find the knowledge you need to take your practice to outstanding heights.

In the next chapter, I'll show you the system that I used to make this happen. So without further ado, let's see what goes into becoming a truly successful doctor.

CHAPTER 2

How I Generated $374,000 in Profit in One Year Using the System I'm About to Show You

In the previous chapter, I gave you a basic understanding of what it means to run a thriving practice. And now, it's time to get into the system that makes it happen.

How do I know that it does?

Well, that system made one of my practices $374,000 in pure profits within the first year! And as you'll see throughout this book, I'm far from the only one who saw fantastic results from it.

I call it the 7 Figure Stairway System, and I've used it to grow multiple clinics to great heights.

So, let me dive deeper into the improvements I got with that one clinic I mentioned. It's a South Charlotte practice that helps men with erectile dysfunction.

When we opened the clinic, we decided to run newspaper ads. Now, you don't have to do it to succeed, but it just made sense for us. Our target audience is older men, so newspaper ads were an ideal approach.

The point here is that you must have a clear message that you'll aim at a specific audience. In our case, the message hit the nail right on the head. It reads:

"Have you these symptoms of erectile dysfunction? Over 322 million men worldwide will suffer from erectile dysfunction at some point in their life."

So we knew that our target market was men aged 40–70, 52% of which suffer from this problem. Our message raised awareness of the issue and encouraged the audience to find a solution.

Our solution was a $199 package that included an exam, doctor review, and a test dose. And the campaign we used to sell it achieved astonishing results. Here are the results:

In the first ten days, we collected $70,000 in upfront revenue!

Better yet, the results kept getting stronger with each passing month. For instance, in March, we did $149,000 with $10,000 in monthly recurring revenue. But the crazy thing was that we did so in only three weeks as there was a big snowstorm that made us close for a week.

April was our first full month without any issues that made us close up the clinic. And in that month, we did over $200,000! We collected $176,000 in upfront sales and $24,000 in monthly recurring revenue.

Financial Reports Use the Date Selector to the right to specify date ranges.

Dashboard > Financial Reports

MAY 1, 2014 - MAY 31, 2014

Individual Reports DO NOT include refills.

Counselor Name	ACE %	Number of Tickets	Total Paid	AVG Down Payments	AVG Ticket Amount	Gross Sales	Collected From Balances
[redacted]	10.53%	86	$68,601.00	$1,201.95	$1,404.44	$80,143.00	$5,430.47
[redacted]	0%	1	$0.00	$0.00	$0.00	$0.00	$0.00
[redacted]	6.38%	69	$42,557.00	$905.47	$1,269.96	$59,688.00	$6,339.56
[redacted]	16.67%	13	$4,030.00	$671.67	$671.67	$4,030.00	$709.20
[redacted]	11.86%	83	$50,806.00	$861.12	$1,043.75	$61,581.00	$8,582.56
TOTALS:		257	$165,994.00	$645.89	$799.39	$205,442.00	$21,271.79

Unassigned Tickets

If you look at the numbers for the first half of our year, you'll see why the framework is so powerful. From January 21st to the end of June, we generated $880,000 in upfront payments! Moreover, we secured $87,000 in monthly recurring revenue!

And if that's not enough, the overview of the whole year should be. By the end of our first year, we made over $2.1 million in revenue! And we did $192,000 in monthly recurring revenue!

Now, there's a good reason why the second half of the year was more successful than the first. Somewhere around June, we introduced some high-ticket offers.

Now, this made us take our eyes off the monthly recurring revenue for a moment. But it paid off massively, as those high-ticket offers added a lot to our bottom line.

Initially, we sold those high-end packages for $6,000. Over time, we managed to increase the price in our future clinics to $10,000.

Our first big-ticket offer was platelet-rich plasma. We used it to treat erectile dysfunction, venous leakage, and Peyronie's disease. We then created another offer focused on hair restoration. It didn't do fantastically at first, but the results were decent. However, over the next couple of years, it became one of our strongest offers.

All in all, we generated $374,000 in profits in just one year! And that happened thanks to the framework that I'll give you in this book.

Now, I know what you may be thinking – it was my clinic and my framework. As I actually created the whole system, you might assume that it only applied to my specific situation.

But that's not the case! The framework is suitable for doctors from many different areas, and it's replicable for different practices.

But don't take my word for it. Let me show you another example of what the 7 Figure Stairway System can do.

It's Not Just Me Who's Succeeding with This!

Before Dr. R came to me, his business was doing pretty fine. He ran a clinic in a rural area of the Upper Midwest. The clinic did functional and restorative medicine, and it was generating around $30,000–$45,000 per month in revenue.

Now, this was a decent result that many doctors would be happy with. But the issue was that this revenue wasn't stable; it would ebb and flow from month to month.

As a result, Dr. R couldn't nail down the patterns that ensured satisfying results. He didn't really know where the money was coming from.

Because of this, our first task was to set up a tracking system. I find this to be a critical part of success, as it allows you to truly understand your business.

How so?

The thing is, every doctor wants to boost their conversions and get more patients. But you can't do this if you don't have a clear overview of your current numbers.

Some of the most important metrics doctors must track are acquisition costs and revenue per transaction. You should know exactly how much it will cost to get a patient on board, and how much money they'll bring in.

When you know these numbers, you can then set an appropriate ad spend.

But the issue that I see often is that doctors do it in reverse. They change their ad spend without having this clear overview of the numbers in place. And Dr. R had done the same before he came to me.

We fixed this issue and set clear goals that we'd strive for. Dr. R wanted 70% of calls to result in an appointment. And he wanted to convert 50% of those appointments.

To make this happen, we went through the stages that I'll show you in the following chapters. We needed to:

1. Have a clear offer
2. Excite prospects
3. Educate them
4. Convert them

I'll get into all of these steps in greater detail throughout the book. But for now, let's focus on conversions, as that was the ultimate goal. And the process of converting prospects into patients was pretty straightforward.

We found that a bulk of Dr. R's patients came through a webinar. So, in the webinar, we put a clear offer for either regenerative or functional medicine. Both offers made good money in average revenue per transaction, exactly $2,800.

On the webinar, Dr. R gets a 30% show rate. And for every 10 patients that get to an appointment, he'd sell one or two. On top of this, we also know that it costs around $375 to get each patient.

So for every $375 that Dr. R spends on acquisition, he makes $2,800. Pretty good ROI, right?

Well, with this information, we figured out the only thing that Dr. R had to do in order to start seeing more patients:

Increase his marketing spend.

Yes, that's it!

Once we started doing this, we saw fantastic results. Dr. R wanted to see 70% of people convert to an appointment, and the actual rate was 83%. Instead of a targeted 70% show rate for webinars, we achieved 92%.

Most importantly, the target for appointment conversions was 50%, and we saw 62%!

Right now, Dr. R's marketing spend is around $5,000 a month. Next month, we'll up it to $7,500. And the month after, we'll go to $10,000.

We're going to continue with these increases until Dr. R sees a monthly revenue of $84,000, or around a million per year.

And that's the power of understanding your numbers. Once you do, the path towards growth presents itself. Who would've thought that the only thing Dr. R had to do to surpass his goals was to simply increase his marketing spend?

Well, you can achieve the same with the framework that you'll see in this book. But to do it, you must truly know your business. Get clear on your metrics, and everything else will be much smoother.

Are You Ready to Grow Your Practice?

As you saw, the 7 Figure Stairway System helped me achieve fantastic success with my practices. In the very first year, we've gotten the kind of results that many doctors dream of.

This goes to show that achieving your goals is more than possible. The same methods that helped me are now letting Dr. R take his practice to a whole new level.

The best part is, he doesn't have to rely on any sales tactics that doctors usually consider sleazy. I know how uncomfortable it is to pitch your offer to a patient. But with this system in place, there's no need for this! All the heavy lifting gets done by the time a prospective patient books an appointment.

The outcome is a process that involves much less effort or pressure on either side. The patient doesn't feel like you're trying to sell them something, and you don't feel that way, either. Prospects go through the stages smoothly, and you can convert them without struggles.

But as mentioned, this can only happen once you've gained a detailed understanding of your numbers. I helped Dr. R do it, and it made a world of difference to his results.

So, do you know or track the numbers that I've mentioned? If not, now would be the perfect time to start. And when you do, you can start leveraging the power of the system that I'll discuss in the next chapter.

CHAPTER 3

The 7 Figure Stairway System

I get that, as a doctor, you just want to be able to do your best work and help people. However, this doesn't mean that you shouldn't understand the fundamentals of running a business.

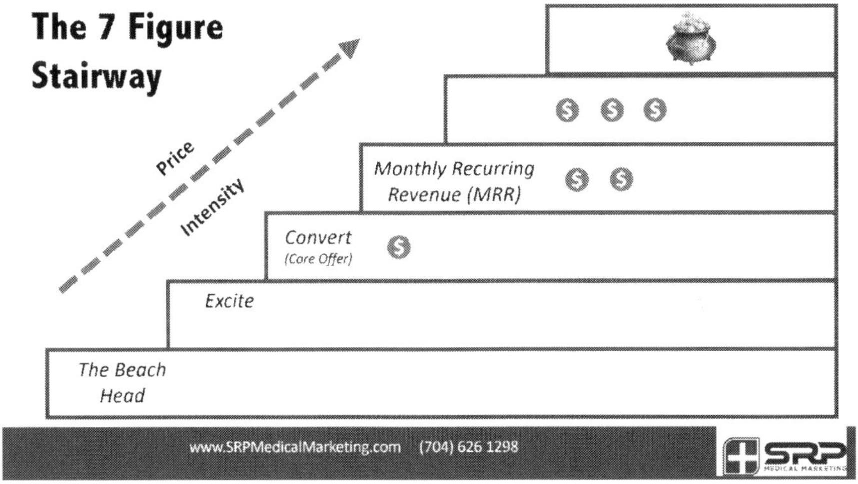

The good news is that you don't need to know or do anything over the top. But you do need to build the right foundation if you want to grow your practice.

Think of this as seeing a patient for the first time. You need to evaluate them and do all the relevant analyses.

Once you do, you can go ahead and make the right medical decisions.

Now, you already know how to do this as a doctor. And I'm about to teach you how to do it as a business owner.

But what is the foundation that you need to build?

It's all a part of my 7 Figure Stairway System that I introduced.

It comes down to the four critical parts, with each of them contributing to your success in its own way.

So, without further ado, here's what the framework consists of:

1. Beachhead

How well do you understand your market? Do you know exactly who your target audience is? Are you sending a message that truly resonates with them and provides an offer that matches their needs?

In most cases, doctors don't really have all these things in place. And yet, they're essential to success.

Now, you might think that you have a clear offer that suits your target market. But let me ask you something:

Are you hitting at least $100k a month in revenue?

If not, I bet you actually *don't* have such an offer. In my experience, doctors who structure their offer correctly should be hitting this number without any hassle.

And this is what my Beachhead concept is all about. It's that basic offer that works on your front end and will bring you patients that you'll treat in the long run.

In case you don't know, beachhead is a military concept that serves as a perfect metaphor for your offer. It's what allows you to build a base of operations. So if you think of the South Pacific War or the invasion of Normandy, the beachhead was at the forefront of everything.

This is exactly how your offer should work. And for this to happen, you must get crystal clear on your market and message.

Your market relates to the one specific thing that you're doing for a patient. My practice helping people with erectile dysfunction is a perfect example of this.

Now, within your market, you'll have sub-categories of people who need what you have to offer.

In our case, these were:

- Elderly, retired men
- Those with medical difficulties related to surgery or medication
- The general population suffering from erectile dysfunction

As you saw in my story, we crafted a clear and simple message that resonated with our audience. And this allowed us to attract many patients to our clinic.

At the same time, the offer that we structured could meet their needs perfectly.

So this is what a beachhead is in a nutshell. Of course, I'll devote a specific chapter to it, along with the other key factors. For now, let's move onto the overview of the second vital aspect of the framework.

2. Excite

Do you feel like you have a great offer, but you need more people to know about it? Have you tried running campaigns or hiring an agency to do it for you, only to see leads that don't convert?

If so, you're not alone, as this is a very common issue that doctors face. They feel like they have to struggle way too hard to bring new patients on board. Doing so often requires a whole lot of selling, oftentimes with poor results.

What is the reason for this?

It's actually quite simple – you don't have a system that excites your prospects. There's no funnel that they'll go through and warm up until they're ready to buy.

I want you to know that you don't have to be a good salesperson to attract and convert leads. Doctors usually aren't fantastic salespeople to begin with. And yet, I see many of them getting patients left, right, and center.

How?

By having a clear campaign made up of high-quality content that people engage with.

By this, I don't mean some academic or medical content. What I'm talking about is plain, simple content that hits the nail right on the head in terms of the message.

When you combine such content with the right funnel, you can achieve incredible things. And I'm speaking from my own experience here.

For one of my clinics, I built a specific funnel that targeted the right audience. People would find out about us through the web and reach out. And by the time they did, they'd be ready to book an appointment. They basically called to book themselves in! No sales efforts or struggles – just a smooth way of filling up the lead pipeline.

Don’t you want the same? How would you feel if patients came to you ready to go?

I bet running your clinic would be a much more enjoyable experience, right?

Well, I’ll teach you what it takes to make this happen in one of the following chapters, where I’ll dive deeper into exciting your audience.

3. Convert

As you'll learn in this book, all of the components of the 7 Figure Stairway System should work together. This is how you can truly make your results skyrocket and tap into your clinic's full potential.

But just by going through the previous two steps the right way, you'll instantly see massive improvements. If you set it all up correctly, you should be able to convert at least 50% of your first appointments into treatment.

Yes, 50% right on the spot!

If you don't hit this number, it's a clear sign that you haven't checked all of the above boxes. Because with these systems in place, converting 50% of your first appointments should be a piece of cake.

And again, you won't have to actually pitch your leads and feel like a sleazy salesperson in any way. The whole point of the framework is to create a system that will do all that hard work for you.

The outcome that you should see is that people come to your clinic knowing that you can help them. If this happens, they'll convert themselves for the most part.

But what is the real-life impact of making the changes that I'm talking about?

Well, just recently, I worked with a client who had a regenerative medicine clinic. When he came to us, his conversion rates were only 10%.

It didn't take us a long time to pinpoint the exact cause of his struggles. We almost immediately realized that he left $12,000 on the table in just one week. Multiply it by four weeks, and you get $48,000 just sitting there.

Just by making these simple adjustments, we made sure that the client starts bringing in all that money. And since he's already at $60k/month, we'll get him to over six figures just through these simple changes.

So what is your current conversion rate? Are you close to hitting that 50% milestone? If not, know that there’s a simple solution for your troubles.

But this still isn’t enough to let you build the lifestyle you deserve and take your clinic to great heights. That’s why there’s another critical component of the framework that I’d like to discuss.

4. Monthly Recurring Revenue

As I mentioned, everything in the 7 Figure Stairway System should work nicely together to create a strong synergetic effect. If you make this happen, you should be able to get over $100,000 per month in revenue.

But as the name of the framework suggests, your goal is to get to $200k. So how do you get there?

Well, the fourth key stage is to create a stream of recurring monthly revenue.

You can do this in all sorts of ways. Think of it as a health club or Netflix. Instead of one-off sales, you get patients that keep coming back month after month.

This way, you'll even out the peaks and valleys of your cash flow. You'll have a stream of cash that you can rely on.

I can tell you about many doctors who've made this happen with great success. The first one that comes to mind is a client of my friend, who opened his med spa in more than 20 locations. The spa offers laser hair removal, which then converts into multiple streams of recurring revenue. People opt-in for more hair removal, Botox, and a bunch of other things.

The results?

That doctor is making low seven figures *per month, per location*.

Now, I get that this might seem like an unachievable goal. But it's really not! Plus, it only proves that generating tens of thousands is much easier than it seems!

Within the first six months, you should be able to make $25,000 in monthly recurring revenue. The figure should grow to $40,000 within the first year.

Now, this alone would be enough to help you achieve many of your goals. But it's still not $200k, is it?

Well, to really climb the Stairway all the way to the top, there are two more steps that you should take.

Let's focus on that six-month period when you're making $25,000 in recurring revenue on top of the $100,000 that I mentioned. How do you bridge this $75,000 gap in the fastest way possible?

There are two extra steps that you can take to make this happen.

Your High-Ticket and 5% Offer

If you haven't already, you must structure a high-ticket offer for your clinic. And generally speaking, around 30% of those who convert into your core offer should move up to the high-end option. For instance, if you're seeing 80 patients a month, 24 of them should buy the high-ticket offer.

For the sake of simplicity, let's say that your high-end offer costs $2,000. In this case, you'd make an additional $48,000 on top of the existing $125,000, so $173,000 in total.

And to cross that $200k threshold, you'll do one final thing – create what I call the 5% offer.

As the name implies, this offer will target only the top 5% of your patients. It's that massive offer that should exceed $10,000 or so.

When I did this with my clinic, we'd close around two to four of these 5% deals. So again, for simplicity's sake, let's assume that you close three, generating another $30,000 in revenue. Add this to the $173,000 you already have, and you'll total at $203,000!

So this is essentially how the 7 Figure Stairway System works. In the future chapters, I'll expand on each of these four components to show you what it takes to add them to your clinic.

Build the Right Foundation

Hopefully, you now have a better idea of how I managed to achieve such success with my clinics. As you can see, it all comes down to getting a few key things right. Once you do, you can completely transform your clinic.

I've shared a few stories of my clients who've made this happen, and I will share many more. You'll get a chance to see many examples of the framework in practice and the results that it can achieve.

Over the next four chapters, I'd like to devote special attention to each of these components separately. By doing so, I'll show you how you can replicate these processes and build a solid foundation for growth.

As I explained, the first and most important part you need to get right is your Beachhead. In the following chapter, you'll see how to nail it down.

CHAPTER 4

The Beachhead

Let me tell you a story of Dr. B, who achieved massive success with the 7 Figure Stairway System.

When we first met, Dr. B focused primarily on the insurance side of his business. However, he knew that there was a great opportunity on the cash-based side.

Dr. B realized that he couldn't make any more money from the insurance side of the clinic. But he also didn't know how to grow the cash-based side. Because of this, he reached out to me for help.

At that point, he was doing around $250,000 per year. And his goal was to start generating $80,000 per month. While it was surely an ambitious goal, it was more than achievable. All we had to do was figure out the direction in which the business would grow.

Now, Dr. B had way too many things going on at once. He'd jump from one process to the other without any sense of direction. Worse yet, he had to do it all pretty much on his own.

At the same time, Dr. B had to keep up with finances, talk to patients, and treat them. He was also burning through staff, particularly those at the front desk. When a patient would call, they just wouldn't know what to reply.

On one hand, this made sense, as none of the people at the front desk were actual doctors like Dr. B. But this was still a massive challenge that robbed the doctor of time, money, and energy. He just couldn't handle all those different tasks at once.

Luckily, this all changed once we started working together. And identifying the beachhead alone was enough to introduce massive improvements.

You see, we realized that the problem wasn't necessarily cash vs. insurance. Instead, we had to figure out who Dr. B was and who he wasn't. Doing so would allow us to find the right message and the system that we'd build around it.

Soon after Dr. B started working with me, we managed to find his ideal offer – weight loss. This was by far his biggest selling point, as he could get fantastic results for his clients. Dr. B could help them drop 10–12 pounds or lose one to two dress sizes within 30 days.

Once we realized this, we knew that this offer would be Dr. B's beachhead. We also found that 80% of his audience were women. Even though he did work with men and children, this was the audience that we needed to focus on.

And that's what we did. We created a simple yet powerful message that resonated with the target market. The message revolved around losing two dress sizes in 30 days, which was highly appealing to the audience.

Once we clarified the message, it was time to clarify the pathway. We systemized the process that the patients would go through and outlined it clearly.

And finally, we communicated this clear message and pathway to the staff. The ultimate goal of this was to get everyone on the same page and get rid of any confusion or pressure. And this is exactly what happened.

All of a sudden, the staff became much more relaxed. Better still, they started receiving the training they needed. In no time, everyone at the clinic knew exactly what their role was and how to fulfill it.

Consequently, Dr. B was more relaxed, as well. Now that everyone knew exactly what to expect, everything was much more streamlined.

But that's not all. These quick and simple changes gave Dr. B tangible results. Upon making them, he started receiving 25% more calls and appointments.

Naturally, this resulted in the much-needed increase in revenue, which used to be very inconsistent.

After the first month, Dr. B saw an increase of $5,000. By the end of the second month, this turned into $8,000. And then, the clinic started growing exponentially.

This almost always happens once you get very clear on your beachhead. You'll notice incremental changes at first, which will then skyrocket.

And that's the power of knowing your clinic and what it can offer to the market. It allows you to secure a unique position.

Now, you're probably wondering what it takes for you to do the same thing as Dr. B and achieve this kind of result. So let's get straight into it.

The Message, the Market, and the Offer

Let's face it – you're a doctor, not a marketer. They didn't teach you how to run a business in medical school. So when you graduated, you might've found yourself in the position of the unsuccessful doctor from the opening story I shared.

You knew that your practice needed strong marketing. But because you didn't know how to set it up, you did the next best thing – hired a third-party to do it for you.

There's nothing wrong with this, as it's what many doctors do. In fact, it can be a truly powerful way to spread the message and attract patients.

But here's the issue:

Doctors resort to third-party agencies without any understanding of their offer, market, and message. In other words, they don't have their beachhead.

So what happens then?

Well, the agency does what it can. It focuses on the technicalities of marketing. It might craft a message and find the right channel. The agency runs a campaign, and you get a few leads from it.

And then… crickets.

Those leads that come never convert, and you end up wasting money on the agency.

So, is this their fault? After all, they're the experts. They should've created a high-performing campaign, right?

Well, not necessarily.

You see, the marketing agency doesn't know your business as well as you do. And it shouldn't. It's not their job to identify your clear offer and message – it's yours. You need to give this to the agency if you want them to do a good job.

Remember when I mentioned that your beachhead is the foundation of everything? Well, this is what I had in mind when I said that. If you jump to campaigns without clarity, you're dead in the water.

You see, conversions are the result of what I call KLT – know, like, and trust. And a generic agency doesn't spend time on these three things.

So, if you've ever found yourself struggling to run campaigns, this is the reason why. You didn't have a clear message, market, and offer. And because the foundation of your marketing wasn't solid, everything you tried to build on it fell through.

This is where the importance of your beachhead shines. As I explained, it's a military concept where all the resources get concentrated into one specific area. And your own beachhead should do the same. You have to put everything into a specific marketplace and drive all patients into one spot.

You'll do this through a powerful message that cuts through the market noise, thanks to its clarity. The message will reach the right people and compel them with the communicated benefits. And when this happens, your campaigns will be truly successful.

However, there's another common issue that I'd like to address.

Stop Talking About the Machine

How do you communicate your offer? Do you focus on the technical aspect of it?

If so, you're making a common mistake that I see in many doctors.

You see, people don't care about how the machine works. All they want to know is that it can get them the results they need. In other words, you shouldn't focus on your process but its benefits from the patient's perspective.

The best way to explain what this means in practice is by using an example. And I'll refer back to the erectile dysfunction campaign. It was the beachhead that resulted in amazing success for us.

Why? Let's break the campaign down, and you'll see for yourself.

As I mentioned, the key message was:

"Have you these symptoms of erectile dysfunction?"

And yes, I know that the grammar is a bit messed up here, but there's a good reason why I structured it that way – that's how people talk in real life.

Now, this wasn't the entire message. Instead, we had to call out the market. By doing so, we'd show exactly who our offer was for. And we did it by using a simple statistic:

"Erectile dysfunction impacts 52% of men between the ages of 40 and 70."

Would I work with a patient if he was 35 or 73 years old? Of course! But we knew that the vast majority of our target market was in this age bracket, so that's why we included it.

You must do the same for your market. You'll want to leave no room for people to guess if your offer is for them. Rather, you must speak to your specific market clearly and without any confusion.

I did mention a few other things in the ad. I touched on Viagra, as many of our patients reached out to us because it had failed to help them. This further specified the ideal patient that our offer was for.

And as outlined, the offer was a super-clear one:

"The office visit is only $199 and includes your exam, doctor review, and test dose. If you don't see results in the office, you owe us nothing. That's our guarantee to you."

So we found a clear market, message, and offer. In one word, we had a perfect beachhead for our clinic. And you already saw the results that this created.

Of course, a big part of this success was that we focused on the benefits. We didn't overexplain how we could help someone with ED. We only let the audience know that we could fix their problem for good.

So when creating your message, make sure to do the same. People don't want to read a bunch of confusing words that they won't understand. This will disengage them from the campaign, making it very hard to convert. Focus on clarity in all areas of your beachhead, and results will follow.

Figuring Out the Flavor of Gum Your Market Wants

Doctors sometimes believe that they know their target market just because they have the demographics figured out. But this is nowhere near enough.

You need to dive much deeper and know everything about your target audience. This is one of the three main components of the beachhead, and the concept can't work without it.

How so?

Let's say that you have that million-dollar message figured out. As you'll learn, this is a message so strong that people can't resist it. At the same time, you've created a signature system for your target market. You have a unique way of delivering services that people can't find elsewhere.

These are the other two factors of your beachhead. With them in place, your clinic would see some decent results. And the same would happen if you combine any two of these three factors. However, unless you have all three of them in place, you can't tap into your full potential.

Think of these components as overlapping circles. Your success lies at the center of the area where all of them overlap. This is what I call the white-hot business zone.

So, how do you find your specific market and make this happen? Let me explain this with my own story.

The Starving Crowd, the Bleeding Neck, and My $100,000 Mistake

Have you ever heard of Gary Halbert? He was an incredibly famous copywriter who made a fortune during the 70s and 80s.

However, Gary didn't like paying taxes very much. And so, he ended up in federal prison.

While he was there, Gary would send letters about starting a business to his son, Bond. They're called the *Boron Letters*, I recommend you take a look at them when you get a chance.

http://www.thegaryhalbertletter.com/Boron/BoronLetterCh1.htm

But now, there's a particular letter that I'd like to focus on. In it, Gary asked his son what would happen if he had a hamburger stand next to a competitor's. What would he do to destroy the competitor?

Now, when I heard that same question at an event, people would yell all kinds of stuff. They'd suggest secret sauces, sesame seeds, bigger patties, and so on.

And they were all wrong.

There was only one thing that the hamburger stand needed to succeed – a starving crowd.

And that's what you must do as well. I surely did multiple times, though it wasn't always a success.

You see, back in 2004, I was teaching people how to get rich with real estate. A guru would sell a program, and we'd provide coaching. We'd run seminars across the country, and they were highly successful.

At some point, we realized that around 60% of the attendees were Christians.

You're wondering why this was even important, aren't you?

Well, the reason is that this allowed me to find my starving market. Being a Christian myself, I started organizing events where we'd all get together and discuss all sorts of topics.

I realized that there was a lot of room for growth here. I thought that it was my starving crowd, so I decided to take it to the next level.

I created a website and started running the whole thing. I ran ads, created a podcast that had 124,000 listens, and did a bunch of other things. Considering all those efforts, I expected it to turn into something incredible.

But instead, it failed miserably.

Why?

Because my starving crowd was broke. I found the people with a need, but they couldn't afford to meet it. And so, I lost $100,000 because I'd failed to consider this factor.

A few years later, a guy by the name of John Paul Mendocha got me into the ED business. And he taught me the concept of the bleeding neck vs. the skinned knee.

Would you go to the ER if you had a skinned knee?

Of course not. You'd just put some Neosporin and Band-Aid on it, and you're good to go.

But if you had a bleeding neck, you'd surely run to the ER instantly. And this is exactly the kind of audience you need. You want those with a bleeding neck that will want to act right away. And this brings me to the next important point that I need to discuss.

Understand the Market's Pain Points

I've seen first-hand what happens when you're clear on your target market. So let me give you an example of my own clinics here.

When we opened a clinic, we started tracking every single marketing avenue. We were spending $60,000 per location to advertise through channels like ESPN Radio, Charlotte Weekly, WRFX, and Fox Sports. For each of them, we tracked calls that patients made as a result of our marketing efforts.

In our second month, we received 379 unique calls. These are the people who'd never called to make an inquiry before. We had 275 unique callers from TV and radio alone.

Now, this was by no means a bad result. But we still had to figure out our target market with greater accuracy.

Little by little, we zeroed in on our market. And just one year later, the results were fantastic.

In one month, we saw 501 unique calls from radio and TV, as opposed to 275 from the year before. We did a little less in newspaper ads compared to the year before, but we still pulled incredibly well.

Outside of these categories, we had 1,163 unique calls from people who'd never called before!

Now, it's worth mentioning that this was in our second location, so that was certainly a factor. But all those results were mostly due to the fact that we finally understood our market's pain points.

We were booking around 85–100 appointments per week in those two locations, so they were truly well-oiled machines. After we understood our market fully, they achieved astonishing success.

But what does it actually mean to gain clarity on your market in such a way?

Creating an Ideal Customer Profile

We all know that demographics are important for understanding your market. But many doctors don't realize that this is just the basic level. There are many other factors that you need to focus on.

The best way to encompass them all is by creating an ideal customer profile.

Beyond things like your audience's gender, age, marital status, and other basic information, you need to know:

- Social media groups
- Experts they follow
- Tools and platforms they use
- Opinions
- Behaviors
- Activities they like

… and many other things.

So, why do you need to go so deep and understand your customer's minds? For example, why would you need to know someone's opinions on stuff like politics?

Well, because all those factors determine how you'll market to your audience. You won't use the same message for someone who voted for Trump and Bernie Sanders. As much as it may seem irrelevant to you, you must know how your audience thinks.

Now there's a very specific component of your customer's profile that you need to focus on – their pain points and frustrations.

You see, everyone wants to move away from pain and achieve pleasure. So what does this look like for your ideal customer? You must know this before you start any marketing efforts.

Let me give you an example of how this all works.

We give names to each of our customer profiles. So let's look at Larry.

We based the Larry persona on an actual client. And I know everything about him. Here are only some of the information I have on Larry:

- 60+
- Widower
- Lives in Charlotte
- Retired, no debt
- Dixiecrat (a conservative democrat)
- A member of senior groups
- Has three kids
- Has no problem falling in love, but doesn't want to upset the kids
- Tried Viagra, but it doesn't help him and gives him a headache
- Misses companionship and having a woman sleep next to him
- Hates getting old and wants more energy

This is only the tip of the iceberg when it comes to Larry's profile. See how detailed it is? All of this data plays a role in my marketing to this customer profile. It allows me to create the perfect message that will resonate with the market.

The next question that I bet you have is, *"Where do I find all this information?"*

So let's answer it.

Get Knee-to-Knee with Your Prospects

What are you currently doing to get to know your audience? And I'm not talking about marginally knowing them. I'm talking about really *knowing* them.

Well, I'd like to share some of the best things that you can do to make this happen.

And the first one is to just ask the right questions and listen to the answers.

You see, people love talking about themselves – you just have to encourage them. The more you do, the more they'll trust you.

So, when you meet a patient, ask them what made them come to you. Whatever their answer, have them tell you more about it. And as they answer, see how you can keep the conversation going.

Your goal here is to get as much information on their pain points as you can. This is how you'll be able to zero in on your market and understand it on a deeper level.

But face-to-face communication is far from the only way to make it happen. Another thing that I strongly suggest is going to Facebook groups. They're a true goldmine of all the information you'll need.

Now, don't go to the groups where doctors discuss different techniques. Instead, join the groups that your audience uses to share their experiences and opinions.

For example, I joined an ED group where people talk about pretty much everything related to the condition. And this gave me a wealth of useful data.

When you join a group, don't use it to sell or do anything of the sorts. Just watch and listen. See what people talk about, and how they feel about their issue. Look at the ways they've tried solving it before. Take some time to truly understand what your market is going through.

No matter what your practice does, there's surely a Facebook group for it. So, find your people online, and closely track what they say and do.

Another fantastic way to get to know your audience is to Google their opinions on what your clinic does. Try "Americans' opinions on anti-aging", for instance. This will uncover all sorts of resources that you can use.

You'll likely find a bunch of articles that discuss how people feel about their problems and potential solutions. You can also look at different content online and see what it discusses. Content that answers questions is particularly useful here.

Why?

Because the answers to those questions need to be in your marketing message. Google will often suggest questions as soon as you type something in, so you can know exactly what your audience wants to learn about.

So, have you ever done any of these things?

If not, I want you to start as soon as you can. All of the information you need is already out there – you just need to know where to look.

Sure, this will take quite some time and effort. But gradually, you'll learn everything you need to know about your market. And when this happens, you'll be ready to craft an ideal message.

Crafting Your Million-Dollar Message

So you've nailed down your target audience. Now what?

Well, it's time to target them with the message that will resonate with them perfectly. In other words, it's time to create your million-dollar message.

But how?

This is a vitally important topic that deserves quite some attention. If you get this right, your practice's success will skyrocket. And if you don't, most of your other efforts will be in vain.

You need to create a message so strong that people will crawl across broken glass to get your solution.

Yes, I know this seems a bit extreme. But it's really what your message needs to do if you want to build a thriving clinic.

So what does it take to make this happen? Here's what you need to do:

1. Have a Solution to the Bleeding Neck

I already explained that you need to find an audience with a bleeding neck as opposed to a skinned knee. But that's just the first step. The next is to offer a solution that your audience will desperately need.

If I have a bleeding neck, I'll leave everything I'm doing to get to the ER as quickly as possible. I'd want them to fix the problem right away, and I won't worry about how much it will cost me.

And that's exactly what your solution should look like. You need to attract people in such a way that the only thing that matters is getting the fix they need from you.

I'll dive deeper into this a bit further down this chapter. But for now, all you need to know is that you must position yourself as someone who can cure your audience's bleeding neck. And doing so involves something that every doctor should know how to do:

2. Think about the Prospect

Most doctors talk way too much about themselves and their solution. They think that doing so makes them an authority that people will trust.

But guess what?

This doesn't work!

What you need to do instead is focus entirely on your prospect.

The best way to do this is best explained by something I read in a Blair Warren book. It's a 50-page book, but it's chock-full of incredible knowledge. If you need something to read after you've finished this one, I strongly recommend it.

In the book, Warren says something that's a cornerstone of creating a successful message:

"People will do anything for those who encourage their dreams, justify their failures, allay their fears, confirm their suspicions, and help them throw rocks at their enemies."

These five components will be the foundation of your message. Think of them as checkboxes that your message needs to tick. If you do it right, you'll have your million-dollar message. So, let's break down these factors.

Firstly, what do your prospects dream about?

In the case of my prospects, it was the ability to have sex again. ED stopped them from enjoying something that just about all humans need.

Of course, this will vary according to what your practice offers. It might be to live a pain-free life, play with their kids, look beautiful, and so on.

The point is, you must have a crystal clear understanding of your prospect's dreams. But this is only the beginning.

The next thing you must do is justify their failures for not achieving that dream outcome. For instance, my audience suffered greatly because other

ED solutions wouldn't help. Cialis and Viagra have a huge failure rate, around 60% or so.

My job in this context was to show people that it's not their fault that they can't enjoy sex. Instead, it was the fault of those solutions that overpromised and underdelivered.

It's almost certain that your audience tried solving their problem in other ways before coming to you. And all efforts to make this happen resulted in failure. You must justify this failure and show that there's still a chance for your prospects to fix the problem.

At the same time, you need to allay their fears by really tuning into them.

You can assume what fears my audience had. They'd fail with Viagra, and think that it meant they couldn't have sex again. Or they might have to go with implants, which is a horrible option. It can result in infections and all sorts of terrifying complications.

In my clinic, we always allayed those fears before moving onto our own solution. It was a crucial part of our message, and the same will go for your own messages.

But in tandem with this, you must confirm all the suspicions that your audience has around the possible solutions to their problems.

In our example, the suspicions were that Big Pharma keeps selling these ineffective solutions to get people hooked on expensive drugs.

And it's absolutely true! Viagra and Cialis combined made Big Pharma around $20 billion. And drug companies don't care if someone will have sex or not. They just want to keep making these insane amounts of money.

Similarly, a doctor will surely encourage a patient to have implants, since they go for $15,000. And the doctor makes $9,000 in pure profit.

Will the implant work? What will the aftermath be?

The doctor doesn't care!

Of course, patients are intelligent enough to know this, or at least suspicious about it. And we made sure that our message highlights this kind of suspicion.

And finally, your message needs to help the prospect throw stones at their enemies. Of course, the enemy here is your prospect's pain points and all their consequences.

For example, if your audience has knee issues, the enemy might be the weight that they're putting on because they can't exercise. Or they might not be able to enjoy their favorite activities.

If your prospect deals with afternoon brain fog, the enemy is the possibility for them to lose their high-paying job.

I could throw in a bunch of other examples. But you get the idea. And one of the key goals of your marketing message is to help the prospect throw rocks at their enemy.

So, no matter the kind of message you're creating, it must contain these five factors. If you follow this formula closely, your campaigns will instantly become so much more effective. But of course, your work doesn't stop there.

3. Show Them the New Opportunity

The ultimate goal of your message is to draw people in and make them see that your solution is the one and only. For this to happen, you must show your prospects an entirely new opportunity to fix their pain.

Why?

Because they've likely tried all sorts of things. And with each failure, they lost more and more hope. They've grown more skeptical, which makes them less open to certain solutions. If you position yourself as yet another of those solutions, your messages won't convert.

So, once you know exactly what your prospect dreams about, you need to show how you can get them there. But it must be something that they haven't seen before.

You're not just going to say that you offer stem cell therapy, HRT, or another solution. A bit later in this chapter, I'll show you everything you need to know about naming your offer the right way.

But for now, you must understand that your audience needs something innovative and out of the box.

Now, I know what you're thinking:

"But aren't there 20 other regenerative medicine clinics that offer the exact same thing I do?"

This might be true. However, you need to let the prospect know that nobody holds the secret to their dreams but you.

Russel Brunson explains this perfectly. In his words:

"If I can get someone to truly believe that the new opportunity is key to what they want the most, and they can get it only through my vehicle, then they have no other option but to buy."

And this is ultimately what you want to do. You want your audience to see that no competitor can do what you do.

In our clinic, the new opportunity was the guarantee that we offered. We promised that we'd give the patient a test dose, and if it didn't work, they didn't owe us anything. And that's what appealed to so many people who needed a new solution to their ED problem.

No matter who your audience is, this is what they truly expect from you. So, get clear on their desire, and then show a new way of making it a reality.

4. Show Them the New Mechanisms

If you go out and say, *"I run a regenerative clinic,"* you'll get nowhere. There are hundreds of clinics that can say the same, so you'll all get lost in this sea of generic messages.

To truly succeed, you must come up with your own mechanism that you'll sell. And then, you need to communicate that mechanism through your messages.

Does this mean that you have to create entirely new processes and methods?

No! It just means that you need to package what you're already doing into a system.

An ideal example of this is P90X. It's an exercise-at-home program that went on to generate billions of dollars.

And yet, home exercise programs had existed for decades before it showed up. And so did the main concept that the program relied on – muscle confusion. It means that you change up your exercise routine so that you avoid the muscle plateau effect.

So none of the concepts of the P90X program was innovative. And yet, people bought the program like crazy.

Why?

Because it encompassed the whole process and addressed all the key areas of a unique offer. The program's belief was:

"Avoiding the muscle plateau effect (new opportunity) *is the key to building muscle* (the desire), *and it's only available through the P90X muscle confusion system* (the new mechanism)."

We did a similar thing in our ED clinic. We talked about avoiding the testosterone plateau as the key to getting back one's sexual desire. And we made sure the audience knew that it was only available through our solution.

Proactiv used the same formula for their solution:

"Attacking acne at every stage of the cycle (new opportunity), *is the key to keeping your skin clear and healthy-looking* (the desire). *And it's attainable only through Proactiv combination therapy* (the new mechanism)."

Sure, Proactiv might've come up with some new lotions and solutions. But for the most part, their success was due to the entire system that they sold. And you need to do the same thing with your offer.

On top of this, you really want to dive deep into the desired outcome. We used our message to show prospects everything that they can achieve with our solution beyond a healthy erection:

- Increased sex drive and pleasure for both partners
- Better sleep
- Better performance at work
- More energy
- Quicker weight loss

... and so on. By using this formula, we achieved astonishing success. And so can you.

To make it happen, you need to do the three things that summarize everything I've talked about so far in this chapter.

First, you need to understand your prospect's desire. Never try to formulate a message or solution based on rational thinking or logic. This isn't what gets people to buy – emotions do.

People buy products, make massive decisions, and even join cults purely based on desire. There's little to no room for logic here.

For example, I love driving a Mercedes, much like many people do. I know that a Hyundai Genesis is a great car, but I still won't choose it over a Mercedes, as I love how driving it makes me feel.

When it comes to all purchase decisions, this is how your audience thinks. And you must play to this emotional framework if you want to sell effectively.

The second thing you must do is show why your process is unique. Don't just say that you do stem cell therapy. This won't set you apart from the crowd. Rather, you must create your own process and make it different from all others.

And finally, you must name your process uniquely. You wouldn't believe the difference that doing so can make. And since this is a topic of its own, it deserves a section of its own.

Developing (and Naming) Your Signature Solution

In the previous section, I explained that you must create a new mechanism for solving your audience's problems. In other words, you need a unique signature system.

What you're looking to do here is create an entire ecosystem of processes that deal with all your patient's pain points. You then unite all those processes into a system that you'll offer to them.

I can share tons of examples of successful signature systems. So let's start with mine.

In my ED clinic, I had a system that I called the Stairway to Sex Heaven. My goal was not just to help my patients with ED. Instead, I wanted them to live a better life and fix all the consequences of this issue.

The first stage of the system was in relation to performance. My patients wanted more than just an ability to get an erection. They also wanted predictable performance so that they know they'll be able to enjoy sex whenever they wanted.

Now, when someone could ensure predictable performance, they wanted to increase their desire. This didn't apply to everyone, but a significant portion of our patients wanted it. Because of that, the second stage was all about helping the patient boost their sex drive. We could help them enjoy sex more and feel younger as a result.

But do you know what goes hand in hand with feeling younger?

That's right – looking younger.

This is why the third and final stage was largely about cosmetic changes. Some patients wanted hair restoration, others wanted Botox, and so on. But the point is, we wanted to help people completely change the way they feel and look.

Now, only around 10% of our patients actually went this far. But that was fine, as I already explained how our system worked. That offer was specifically designed for that exclusive group of patients in the first place.

So when someone came to our office, we outlined the entire system in front of them. We'd go through all the stages to show patients what outcome they could achieve.

Of course, not everyone needed all our solutions. Some patients would only choose one, while others would opt-in for all three.

But the point is, what we sold wasn't a one-off process or transaction. It wasn't about the patient coming in and just getting pills or something like that. Rather, we took them on a journey and showed them what they could achieve.

This is exactly what your signature system needs to do. You need to have a comprehensive solution that consists of different processes your patients need.

You can do this no matter what your package is. Just look at my friend Perry Marshall, who uses the same method for his Google AdWords offer.

Perry has three components of his signature system called the Tactical Triangle:

- T – traffic
- C – conversions
- E – economics

So basically, if you work on your traffic, you'll have more conversions. This allows you to work more on your economics and pay more for getting even more traffic, which then results in more conversions. It goes around and around like a flywheel.

Of course, there's much more to the concept, but this is just a basic idea. Perry offers a system of processes that helps his clients dominate Google AdWords marketing. Each component contributes in some way, and they achieve astonishing results when combined.

I showed you this example to let you see that you can structure any offer this way. Whatever you're selling, you can (and should) build a signature system out of it.

But how?

Well, it all comes down to the things that I already discussed. You need to know your patients' desires, understand your beachhead, and come up with a new mechanism. This essentially summarizes all the important points I've made so far in this book.

What I suggest you do is very simple:

Go to PowerPoint and, under the Insert tab, you'll see Smart Art. There you'll find a bunch of different graphs that will let you visualize your processes. Choose one, and then come up with the ecosystem that you'll offer.

Make sure to have at least three different levels. If you have a fourth, great. But if not, don't worry about it. Nail down the three core levels first, and then you can come up with the fourth one eventually.

So, what phases could you include in your offer? Give this a serious thought, and then experiment with different mechanisms until you create the one that you're happy with. Once you do, it's time to put a nice bow on it by naming the system in an attractive way.

Naming Your Signature Process

The process I'm describing in this book is the 7 Figure Stairway System. I used a similar name in my ED clinic with the Stairway to Sex Heaven framework.

And if you look at just about any successful offer out there, you'll see that it features such an appealing name.

The reason for this is obvious enough. You need to grab people's attention from the moment they hear about your offer.

They need to see the benefits right from the get-go.

For instance, compare the "Stairway to Sex Heaven" to "testosterone pellets".

You can see how the latter sounds so much drier and more boring. Plus, it's anything but unique, as tons of other clinics do the same thing.

This is why you can't just say that you're performing a certain procedure or therapy. You need to name it in such a way that the outcome is perfectly clear.

So how do you do it?

It's actually not that hard at all! You don't need to be a hugely creative person to come up with a catchy name.

What I recommend is to simply go to Amazon and find the best books on how to name a business.

All you have to do is type this into the search field, and then find the books with the most positive comments.

Look for books with a lot of reviews, and choose the top three options.

Then, set aside some time to go through these books and brainstorm.

As you keep reading, new ideas will keep popping into your brain.

This is how I've done it, and it took me very little time to find an ideal name for my framework.

You can go through the entire process over one weekend. When you do, you'll have a perfect name for your new mechanism.

Create Your System

When doctors struggle, it's almost never because what they do isn't good enough. It's because they haven't found a way to structure and communicate their offer the right way.

By using what you've learned in this chapter, you can make sure that this doesn't happen to you. Remember that it all comes down to how well you know your audience and packaging your offer in a way that appeals to them.

So if you haven't already, now's the perfect time to dive really deep into your prospects' minds. Create detailed customer profiles that let you truly get to know your patient as if they were your best friend.

And then, create a signature system out of the processes and treatments that you offer. Instead of just a transaction, give your patients a chance to go on a journey with you. Think of all the ways in which you can make their lives better, and add them to your system.

If you nail down everything from this chapter, you'll be well on your way towards outstanding success. However, it's still only one piece of the puzzle. And in the next chapter, I'll focus on another key one – exciting your audience.

CHAPTER 5

Excite

Before Dr. S came to me, he'd already developed a highly valuable offer for his target market. It was a high-ticket regenerative medicine offer that sold for at least $10,000.

Having such an offer in place meant that Dr. S could achieve decent success with his clinic. He had a steady patient flow, seeing around two to three patients per day.

However, there were quite some issues that stopped Dr. S from maximizing the performance of his clinic.

Firstly, there was a lot of uncertainty involved. The doctor would find himself in many situations that made him go, "*I have to think about this.*"

There was very little clarity and structure in place, which naturally stunted the practice's growth.

On top of this, Dr. S found that it took four to six months for a patient to convert. Like many doctors, he saw a very low close rate of 10–20% on the first appointment.

When Dr. S joined me, we saw a great opportunity in his practice. If he could boost his close rate from 20% to 40%, he'd make an additional $16,000 per month. But the question was, how do we do that?

And the answer became perfectly clear once I took a look at the clinic's practices:

We had to find a way to educate and excite prospects before they come in. This way, they'd be ready to get started when they first show up at the clinic.

Now, Dr. S had no processes that would make this happen. He had a CRM platform, but he almost never used it. He also didn't create any kind of content that would keep people engaged until they come to the office.

As you can imagine, this was the first thing that we had to work on. And in no time, we found the ideal solution.

We found a two-week gap between the moment a patient books an appointment and comes to the practice. We decided to fill this gap to nurture the patient as soon as they complete the booking process.

How?

The first thing we set up was a campaign that would educate prospects and let them hear success stories. So, before the visit, they'd receive emails discussing what they can expect once they come. They'd get a welcome email followed by different educational emails.

The second thing we did was offer prospects a video outlining everything Dr S. can offer at his practice. And finally, we included three testimonials that we'd send out.

All of this would happen before someone comes to the clinic. With that campaign in place, it was time to focus on what would happen *during* the visit. And our solution was simple, yet highly effective.

When a patient came to the office, they got some paperwork to fill out. And then, they went into a room to watch a 10-minute video. The video discussed everything they could expect along with another three testimonials.

Plain and simple, right?

Well, this small addition actually boosted conversions from 20% to 55%, as opposed to the target of 40%. And it resulted in an immediate increase of $20,000.

However, this was around the time when the COVID-19 pandemic hit, and people couldn't visit the office. But this didn't stop us from going forward. We just made the entire campaign digital. We leveraged telemedicine to show people the same content they'd watch in the appointment room. And this gave us another increase from 55% to 60%.

Now, you might think that this is a pretty modest increase. But 5% can make a bigger difference than you might assume. Think of it as giving yourself a 5% raise.

But of course, that wasn't all. We covered what would happen before and during the appointment. The final piece of the puzzle was to figure out what happens after.

This was crucial, as there's one main reason why people don't buy after an appointment – friction. They don't trust you, and they might feel like something's still off.

To deal with this, we created another sequence of emails that addressed people's specific pain points. We kept educating prospects and provided even more testimonials.

And with that, we concluded the entire process. We covered every important aspect, and the results were fantastic. Dr. S is now seeing the conversion that his clinic deserves, and he only keeps progressing.

Do you want to see the same results?

If so, let's start with an essential thing that you must do.

It's Time to Think Differently about Your Campaigns

If you're like most doctors, your marketing probably looks something like this:

You hire a third-party provider to run your ads. You pay them and hope that they'll get your qualified leads ready to go. But when prospects visit, you see that this isn't the case. While you might get some leads, most of them end up going cold.

Why does this happen?

I already touched on this earlier in the book, so let me dive a bit deeper into it.

You see, an agency's job is to get people to your landing page. And then, they'll hope that those leads make an inquiry.

There are two common outcomes here. First, the prospect doesn't even reach out to you, which is obviously the outcome that you don't want.

But the alternative often isn't any better. When a patient reaches out, your staff has to handle the communication. And they're not trained salespeople. Just like you, they're medical professionals who don't know how to convert a lead. And this results in your losing a prospect.

Now, you can't blame your staff for this. I'm pretty sure that even you don't have that much sales training, so you can't expect your staff to be sales superstars.

But in any case, a third-party agency always operates under the assumption that you can close the deal. They feed you leads, and you convert them.

So, what should you do? Should you fill your front desk with top salespeople? Should you become one?

No, this would take an unnecessary amount of time and effort. There's a much better way to fill your pipeline with hot leads and close deals more smoothly.

I'm guessing you've at least heard of a marketing funnel. If not, it's essentially a series of phases that your prospects go through before they're ready to buy. Your job is to grease that funnel so that all of this can happen effortlessly.

How?

There are three key areas that you need to focus on. The first one is the top of your funnel. This is the stage at which people hear about you for the first time. And the way this will happen is through successful ad campaigns.

However, this isn't where your efforts should end. On the contrary – it's only the beginning. You can't expect someone to buy just because they've heard of you. At this point, the prospects still don't like or trust you.

This is why the second stage is to use high-quality content to get people through the middle of your funnel. And by this, I don't mean pushing our research or medical papers. I'm talking about specific content that speaks to your audience, written in plain language.

This kind of content makes you likable and relatable. It shows that you truly understand your prospects and know how to help them. Making your audience feel this way is essential for the success of your content and marketing as a whole.

When this happens, you can move to the bottom of your funnel, which is when people make an inquiry. By the time they do, you should've already built enough excitement and trust through your content.

Provided that you did, converting should be a piece of cake. While there will still be people who will end up leaving, you should be able to close at least 50% of your first appointments.

But do you have such an elaborate way of exciting your audience? If not, it may well be the reason why you're struggling. As you saw in the story of

Dr. S, this was the exact issue that stunted his growth. And once we put the right funnel in place, his practice was transformed.

In this chapter, I'll focus on how you can achieve the same. But first, there's something else that I have to address.

The Challenges You Face When Trying to Get New Patients

I already explained why being too reliant on an ad agency is dangerous. But I want to expand on this further, as I keep seeing doctors who make the same mistakes over and over again.

I get that hiring an agency makes all the sense in the world. After all, you didn't train to get good at marketing. Mastering content, SEO, and other skills you need would be a massive waste of your time and energy.

Because of this, you might've decided to just buy all those skills from someone who promises to be an expert.

But the first problem is, you can never really know if an agency is as good as you believe. Sure, you can look at some testimonials and suchlike. But you're almost always taking some risks here.

However, this isn't even the worst issue. Even if you hire a fantastic agency, you'll simply get someone who's good at ad marketing. You won't get the sales component you need. And we've already established that you likely aren't an incredible salesperson yourself.

So what happens is, an agency does its job well enough. But despite their best efforts, you still don't see the conversions that you wanted. And there's only one reason for this:

You don't have a system that would make this happen.

You see, your clinic needs a system that will seduce the patient, not just market to them. By this, I don't mean that you need to use some sleazy tactics or act like a used car salesman. Instead, you need a system that will simply keep people excited and educated.

In other words, you need to pre-screen, pre-qualify, and predispose patients to do business with you. If your current system doesn't have this, and you're simply replying to what comes to your inbox, you're missing out on a ton of opportunities.

Think of it like dating. Let's say you used a dating app and set up a profile. You find one person that you like, and you hope that you'll get married.

This would result in lots of disappointments, right?

A much better approach would be to find a number of people who've taken an interest with you, qualify them, and then only to the top 20%. This way, you'd find what you're looking for much more quickly.

Well, working with patients works exactly the same!

You shouldn't wait for the stars to align before someone agrees to start working with you. You need a system that will give you a predictable stream of warm leads ready to go. So, let me show you such a system.

The Patients Everyday Model

By now, we've already established the biggest trap that many doctors fall into:

They believe that running ad campaigns is all it takes to gain new customers. When, in fact, this is only one component. And if it's the only one you focus on, you'll create these horrible, unstable systems.

I don't know about you, but I like predictable systems that don't require tons of effort every day. When I build a framework, I want it to keep running itself for the most part.

I bet you want something like this for your clinic.

Well, I'm about to show you a framework that does exactly this. It's reliable, predictable, and it will allow you to keep generating tons of hot leads that will convert easily.

I call it the Patients Everyday model.

Now, I like to give credit where credit is due, so it's worth mentioning that I didn't come up with the system. I adopted it from Kevin Hutto, a friend of mine. He's one of the smartest people in marketing I've ever worked with, and he created the system called Clients Every Day.

When I saw the concept, I loved how it worked, so I adapted it and learned how to use it for clinics. And that's how Patients Everyday was born.

The model consists of three key components that every practice must have in place to succeed:

- Clarity
- Campaign
- Context

Think of these as three overlapping circles. No matter which two you put in place, you'll create something valuable.

For instance, if you're clear on your offer and marketing, and you run campaigns, you'll have what I call a flow of opportunity. If you blend campaigns and context, you'll achieve effortless conversions. And if you've got clarity and context, you can have premium pricing.

Now, all three of these sound very appealing. But to truly transform your practice, you want all of them at the same time. You want to find yourself in the middle of these circles, which is what I call the red-hot business zone.

So how do you make this happen?

Well, you need to understand what goes into each of these components. Once you break them down, you'll know exactly how to create a high-performing system.

I won't get too much into clarity, as I already talked about it in the previous chapter. It all comes down to figuring out your beachhead, which consists of:

- Your market
- Your message
- Your offer

If you achieve clarity in these three areas, you'll have one of the three key pieces of the Patient Everyday model.

When that happens, you need to understand what makes a successful campaign. And of course, the most important thing here to focus on is your content.

As I explained, your content needs to excite, educate, and engage your audience. In one word, your campaigns have to inspire people to take that next step towards a better outcome.

Let me give you an example of this.

In our ED clinic, we found that an average person who visited our website would consume six pages of content. And we had *a lot* of content on the website. We put out videos, written content, and a bunch of other stuff.

We used that content to dispel some common myths about ED and generally educate people on the topic.

But this wasn't the only way we leveraged out content. We also used it to run campaigns that would get people to the website first.

We made this happen through all kinds of channels and tactics. We did Facebook, SEO, videos, TV, radio, and so on. The goal here was to get people to the top of the funnel that I already mentioned.

From there, they'd glide through the middle of the funnel, thanks to the content we created. And at some point, those leads would reach the end of the funnel.

So what happens when they do?

Well, that's where the final part of the model kicks in – context. It's where all the magic happens, but only if you get it right.

Context basically means letting people know why you're the right person for their issues. The examples of this are things like:

"The science behind what we do."

"The cool new machine we have."

"Accreditations and expertise of our doctors."

But here's the issue that I see way too often:

Doctors start with context without nurturing their leads and making them go through the funnel.

They talk about themselves before they get people to like and trust them. And this can be one of the biggest killers of your marketing.

You must nurture your leads with content before you give them context. And when the time comes, you'll provide this context through another three areas:

- Character
- Credibility
- Connection

By character, I don't mean being likable or getting people to trust you. I'm talking about your life stories. You need to show people how you got to where you are today. This allows them to learn more about your background, which can go a long way towards building trust.

As far as credibility goes, I see many doctors who try way too hard to convince patients that they're the expert in their area. When, in fact, this is the last thing you should talk about.

You don't have to go overboard when it comes to talking about your skills, training, and certifications. This means much less to your patients than you think.

What you should do instead is let people talk about their experiences with you. Because at the end of the day, people want to see that you can get them the result they need. And if a patient sees their peer living the outcome they want, there's no better way to build credibility.

And finally, when it comes to connections, know that they're vital to success. And you'll establish meaningful personal connections most effectively by sharing personal stories.

Note that this is different from character, as building character involves sharing stories that largely relate to your practice. On the other hand, connections require meaningful, personal stories that people will relate to.

So if you check these three boxes, you'll have context. Pair it with the other two components of the model, and you get everything you need to grow your practice to outstanding heights:

- A flood of opportunity
- Premium pricing
- Effortless conversions

The Patient Everyday model will ensure that your leads go through the funnel as smoothly as they should. But this doesn't mean that every single person that hears about you will buy.

Instead, the funnel is there to weed out those who aren't ready to work. The end result should be that the top 20% of people are ready to go, as I mentioned earlier in this chapter.

But of course, putting all of this into place doesn't happen overnight. So let me address something that you must really nail down.

Creating Content That Excites Your Audience

So we went over why you have to create engaging and exciting content. I also got into the "how" of it all. And now, it's time to dive into the nitty-gritty details and show you exactly what you can do to keep pushing out such content.

Bear in mind that consistency is key here. You need to keep getting people excited about your content if you want to nurture them. And to make this happen, you need a plan.

In other words, you need a content calendar.

Now, this might seem a bit daunting at first glance. But it's actually super simple.

You'll want to have a spreadsheet calendar divided into weeks. At the top of the spreadsheet, you'll see weeks one to four.

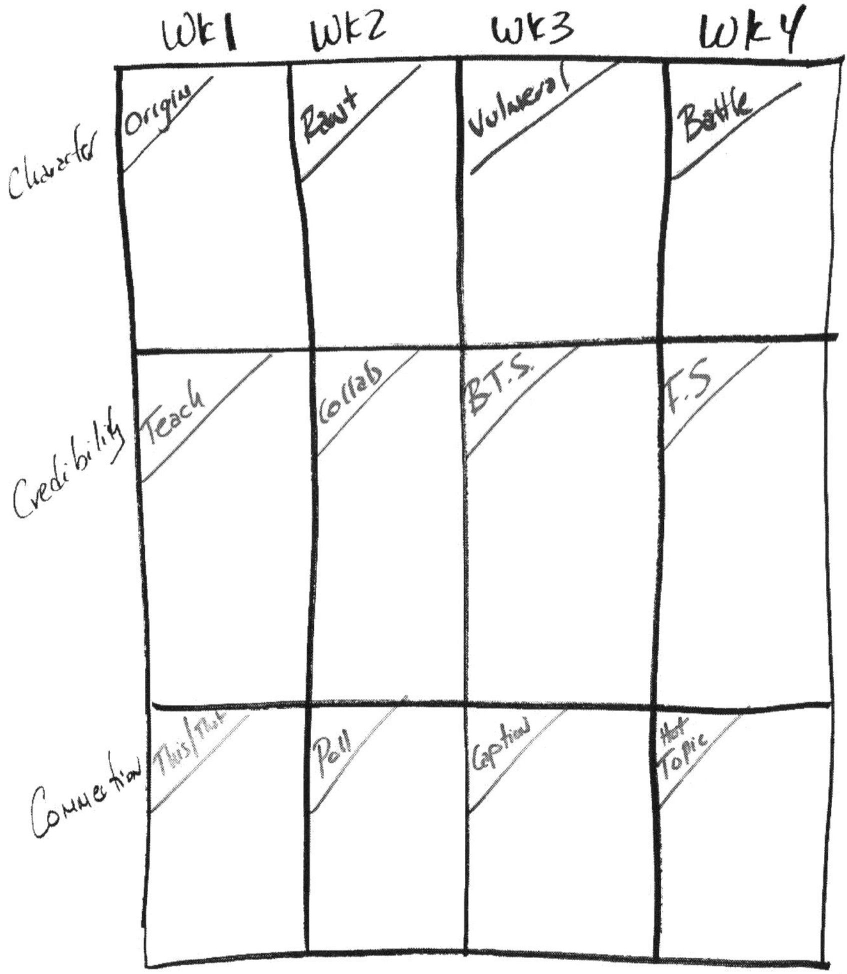

And then, on the left-hand side of the calendar, you need to put in the three factors of context. As a reminder, these are character, credibility, and connection.

When you have this in place, you'll start filling out the calendar with the content that matches these components. For instance, you can create videos of three to five minutes in length. If you do, make sure to put closed captions on it. There are many platforms like rev.com that can transcribe and translate the videos for you.

But what should the videos be about?

Well, for character, I explained that you should share your origin stories. For example, mine revolve around how I got into the ED space. Think about the exciting parts of your journey to owning your practice. Discuss how it all happened, making sure to put in some interesting and engaging stories.

For credibility, you'll want to educate people on your area of expertise and how it relates to their problem. My overarching topics revolved around the science of ED. I did videos like "the Four Horsemen of the Apocalypse", which taught people about the main issues causing ED.

No matter what you do, there are all kinds of stuff that you can teach. Just make sure that the content speaks to your audience's pain and that the language is clear enough for everyone to understand.

As for establishing a connection, you can share all kinds of stories that have nothing to do with your clinic. You can share anecdotes involving your kids, vacation experiences, and a whole bunch of other interesting stuff.

The goal here is to form a deeper relationship with the patient that goes beyond their pain and your clinic. So, come up with engaging topics based on your audience's interest and try to make it fun and inviting.

Other than this, you can create other forms of content that fit into these categories. For instance, I used to do rants on Horny Goat Weed and why it was a bad solution for people with ED. I also created polls that had nothing to do with my clinic, such as who would win the Super Bowl.

On top of this, I talked about my struggles openly to show vulnerability, which goes a long way towards creating strong connections. I also did a bunch of behind-the-scenes videos that educated people on my processes.

As you can see, there are many forms of content that you should make. So, create your calendar and then fill it with the types of content you saw here. With time, you'll systemize the whole process and make it smooth and effortless.

How to Select Your CRM

In the story of Dr. S at the beginning of this chapter, I told you about one of the biggest mistakes that the doctor made. He had a CRM in place, but he didn't really use it.

Now, I've met many doctors who don't even have a CRM, which is obviously even worse. A capable CRM (Customer Relationship Management) platform can do wonders for your funnel. In fact, it's a necessary component of a high-performing funnel.

Why?

Because it allows you to collect all the customer data in one centralized location. You can then use this data to see what works best and what you can do to make your campaigns more effective.

So do you have a CRM in place? If not, you'll want to find one as soon as you get a chance. But how do you know which platform is right for you? After all, there's a plethora of options out there.

You have platforms like MailChimp, which only handles emails. As such, it might lack the features you need to get the most out of your funnel. On the other hand, there are solutions like HubSpot, which are way too complex and have a bunch of options you don't really need. By going with such solutions, you'd overpay for the things that you don't really use.

To make your life easier, I'll just tell you about the two platforms I've used. Both of them hit the nail right on the head when it comes to the features you need and pricing models.

The first one is Kartra, which is a fantastic solution. It's a drag-and-drop platform, meaning that you don't need a whole lot of knowledge to use it. Everything is clean and intuitive, so you should have no trouble getting the hang of how it works.

Kartra shows you a dashboard where you can see your current campaigns and their details. The thing I love about it the most is how easy it is to set up a campaign. You create emails, drag them into the relevant section, and everything happens pretty much on its own. You'll then get all the necessary information about the way your audience interacts with the emails. This allows you to test different campaigns and double down on what works.

You can also create different pages very easily. Again, it all works in a drag-and-drop way, so creating rich pages is quite simple. You can also add those pages to your website without any programming knowledge.

The second platform I use is ClickFunnels, which is an incredibly popular CRM solution. It's mainly geared towards small businesses, and it has just about everything you need to manage your funnel.

It's a more robust solution, so it does come at a higher pricing point of a few hundred per month. But like Kartra, it's a user-friendly platform that makes running your campaigns super easy.

Now, I get that you might not want to bother with all this software on your own. While CRMs are usually not hard to grasp, it still takes some time to get used to them. And the same goes for managing everything.

But the good news is that you don't have to do it alone. In fact, you don't have to do it at all! Let's look at an alternative that many successful doctors choose to go with.

Getting Things Done Quickly and Cheaply – How to Hire on Fiverr

Way too often, doctors try to wear many hats at the same time. And if you've ever done likewise, you know how exhausting it can be. It robs you from focusing on what you do best and makes you work insane hours.

Well, let me introduce a platform that will make sure this doesn't happen – Fiverr.

If you haven't heard about it, it's basically a platform where you can go to get just about anything done for five bucks. Of course, the actual prices will vary depending on the scope of the work you need done. But generally, you can outsource all the work that you don't want to bother with at a very low price.

For example, let's say that you want to start using Kartra. However, you don't want to bother with learning how to set everything up. In this case, all you'd have to do is go on Fiverr and type "Kartra" in the search field.

The search results will be full of amazing virtual assistants that can take care of all the CRM work for you. You can refine your search by setting different filters, budgets, and other options.

Now, you'll find all kinds of different people on Fiverr. Generally speaking, the cheaper you go, the more specific instructions you'll have to provide. This is because those assistants usually reside in countries where the standard is low. As such, English is almost always their second language, so you might run into some language barriers.

However, this isn't a common issue, and I've found that communication issues aren't common at all. For the most part, you can find capable people that will ensure smooth communication via online platforms like Skype.

When looking for freelancers on Fiverr, do your homework and make sure that they can get the job done right. Take a look at their reviews and see if other people are happy with their work. Look at their profile and see if they match everything you need for certain tasks.

Of course, CRM work is only one example of the things that you can outsource. You can do the same for all repetitive or low-value work, or just something that you don’t want to deal with yourself.

So if you haven’t had a chance to explore Fiverr, I couldn’t recommend it more. Find the work that you can get done quickly and cheaply, and let freelancers take it off your plate.

Nurture and Excite Every Lead

Hopefully, you now have a better understanding of why doctors' campaigns often don't work. You can't just focus on the top of your funnel and expect people to convert directly from there. Instead, you need to have a system for warming prospects up until they're ready to work with you.

I know this seems like a lot to take in at first glance. But when you dive into funnel creation, you'll see that the process isn't that taxing. It all comes down to the few fundamental principles that you must follow.

After looking at the Patients Everyday model, how many of its components do you already have? Do they work in the way I explained?

If not, don't worry, as you've just unlocked a wealth of opportunities that you can explore. Sure, it may take some time to set it all up. But once you do, you'll see how easy it is to keep getting warm leads consistently.

Now, exciting your audience makes conversions much easier. But it still doesn't make them happen on its own. It takes a specific set of processes to convert the leads that are ready to go. And I'll tell you all about how to do it in the next chapter.

CHAPTER 6

Convert

It's well-known that all buying decisions are largely emotional. In fact, the vast majority of important life decisions are.

Take marriage as an example. Everyone knows that there's a 55% failure rate. And yet, they still do it.

What doctors often don't understand is that buying anything works the exact same way. Trigger the right emotion, and you're on the money.

Not knowing this, doctors are often way too logical when it comes to selling. After all, their profession calls for this to be the default state. And Dr. Tom from Texas was a textbook example of this.

When he came to me, his clinic was doing fine. It was making around $30,000–$35,000 per month. He and his partner wanted to leave their respective pain medicine practices and go full-time with the clinic.

But the challenge was that they were getting very few conversions. It would often take between four and six months for them to convert a patient, just like Dr. S from the previous story.

So when Dr. Tom came to me, this was his absolute priority. He wanted a system that would give the clinic's conversion the boost it deserved.

To help make this happen, I first introduced my 70:70:50 formula. It means that we want to convert 70% of first-time callers into an appointment. We then want to see a 70% show rate and close 50% once they walk through the door.

Now, Dr. Tom's booking rate was at a nice 40%. Not too bad, but surely nothing to blow your mind. However, it was conversion that was stopping the clinic from further growth. At just 15%, they were nowhere high enough to make the practice expand.

Then, Coronavirus hit, and everything shut down. But Dr. Tom used this time to put a solid conversion system in place and restart on a high note. And he sure did.

The first thing we focused on was putting a script for inbound calls in place. The second thing was me telling Dr. Tom that I expected him to close at least 50% of appointments at the first meeting.

And finally, we set up tracking processes so that we could measure progress. A great thing about it was that Dr. Tom and his partner were highly athletic, so they'd gotten used to tracking performance every day.

After the pandemic settled down a bit, Dr. Tom reopened his practice with a bang. He did $103,000 in his first month of being open! For reference, he did $35,000 that same month one year before.

During the second month, Dr. Tom made $63,000, as opposed to $20,000 at the same time the year before.

And he did all of it by simply following my Big Money Script, which I'll show you further down this chapter.

Dr. Tom's practice saw the conversion rate skyrocket to 83%. And the average procedure went for $3,500. As you can imagine, he and his partner were absolutely thrilled with the results.

This is the power of the script that I gave Dr. Tom, paired with a focus on emotions. Once Dr. Tom understood what truly drives buying decisions, the success of his practice took a massive leap forward.

And the same can happen for you once you get crystal clear on how your people buy.

As with other components of the 7 Figure Stairway System, Convert encompasses a few critical things that you must understand. So let me start with the foundation of it all.

What Is Your Core Offer?

In the previous chapters, I told you everything you need to know about your beachhead and how to excite people. If you do the work that relates to those two areas, you'll have a strong foundation that will boost your ability to convert patients.

However, your core offer will play a critical role here. Without it, you'll leave out one of the main pieces of the puzzle.

But what even is a core offer?

Simply put, it's an offer that converts consistently. It's something that gets people into the system so that they can start knowing, liking, and trusting you.

And no, a core offer isn't about saying how great you are or talking about your machine. Instead, it's just an offer that you can use across different media to keep converting patients into prospects. It needs to get people into your recurring revenue, high-ticket offers, and everything else you're selling.

With this in mind, your core offer should be able to make you at least $100k in monthly revenue.

Now, the good news is that creating a core offer isn't a stretch for most doctors. It's largely about improving what you already do.

But how? What makes a great core offer?

First of all, the offer needs to be simple. It should be something that people can hear in different places and repeat without trying hard to remember it.

For instance, Domino's promises to deliver pizza in 30 minutes tops, or it's free. FedEx offers a guarantee that the package will be there overnight.

These are all examples of plain and simple core offers that people understand and remember without any issues. Of course, there's also a promise within each of them. The benefit to the customer is clearly communicated, which is critical to success. Your core offer should always focus on what the patient will get out of it, not you.

On top of this, you want your core offer to have risk reversal. You want to give people a test drive or something like that.

This is what we did in our ED clinic. Our core offer was coming to the clinic one time, meeting with the doctor, and getting a test dose. And if the patient doesn't see results within 12 minutes, they owe us nothing.

So, we basically promised the patient that we'd get them an erection right there in the office. We obviously didn't word it that way, but that was the message that they'd hear.

Now, your core offer doesn't need to look exactly the same as our example. Depending on the nature of your practice, providing test doses might not be possible. But the good news is that there's a whole bunch of other things that you can offer instead.

I already mentioned that friend of mine who grew his med spa to 20 locations. Well, he'd offer things like $100 Visa gift cards to those who'd sign up for the treatment.

Sure, he could've just knocked off $100 from the treatment in the form of a discount. But this wouldn't have the same power as a gift card. And it's these kinds of nuances that you have to understand when creating your core offer.

On top of this, you can offer many different things as promotional core offers. I've seen doctors do free blood tests, MRI reviews, and other valuable services. But no matter what you do, your core offer must be self-liquidating. In other words, it needs to be able to pay for itself.

So, all in all, you need to have a compelling reason why someone will come to the office, and make sure that it always pays for itself on the spot.

However, there's another dimension to your core offer.

You see, it's not just something that you'll use to convert patients when they come for an appointment. You'll also use your core offer to unlock upselling opportunities.

How does this work?

Think of your core offer as a gateway to either recurring revenue or high-ticket offers. It's like selling marijuana as a gateway drug to heavier options like heroin. Yes, I know that it's a horrible example, but it paints a perfect picture of how your core offer should work from this perspective.

So, you need an offer that works for 80% of your target market. And then, you want a portion of that 80% to progress into a higher-level offer at some point. For reference, you're looking to get 35%–50% of your patients to do this.

But how exactly does this work in practice?

Example – The Buy One Get One Offer

The best way to sum up everything from the above section is by using a simple example. So, let's say that your core offer was "buy one get one free" Botox.

Now, you probably wouldn't make a lot of money on this offer. Depending on your acquisition costs, you might actually *lose* money.

But guess what? That's absolutely fine!

How so?

It's because you're not even supposed to make the most of your money at this stage. Instead, you'll use this offer as a gateway for upsells, which is where you'll actually make money.

Let's assume that you convert 33% of your patients into a monthly recurring revenue or high-end offer. By making this happen, you could make *a lot* of money.

How do I know that?

Because I worked with a clinic that did exactly that! It's a clinic in Sarasota that does tons and tons of Botox. They have a fantastic machine in place, which allows them to see around 20 patients every single day. And 33% of those patients end up in these top-level offers.

The result?

This clinic added $200,000 per month to their bottom line! So even though their core offer didn't make them right, those upgrades to the bigger plan sure did.

Here's another example of our own clinic:

Our core offer sold for $1,100, and we'd see around 35 patients per week. Those 140 patients a month would generate $154,000 in revenue. The upsell plans that we'd get patients in would give us another $25,000 in monthly recurring revenue, which gave us a total of $179,000.

On top of this, we'd get another $25,000–$65,000 per month from our high-end offer. So at the end of each month, we'd land anywhere between $204,000 and $244,000.

With this in mind, our front-end offer was the foundation of everything. ED treatment would lead to hormone replacement therapy. PRP treatment would lead to hair restoration. So, that core offer that we'd put in place would keep sending people to those bigger plans, giving us fantastic results.

Now, there's one more thing that I'd like to go through when it comes to crunching the numbers. On top of everything that your core offer can yield, it can actually help you buy more patients.

How?

I already shared an example of that client who'd leave $12,000 on the table every week. With the systems we put in place, he can now add these $48,000 per month to his clinic. And he can use this money to acquire lots of patients, which would keep the wheel turning even faster and generate even more revenue.

All of this happens just because we were able to fix the client's core offer. And if you can do the same, you can expect incredible results.

Emotion Is the Primary Motive for Buying Decisions

You might not be consciously aware of this, but every buying decision you've ever made was purely based on emotions.

Think about the coat you've bought. Why did you buy it? It surely triggered a positive emotion that made you do it. Sure, you might've purchased it because it was on a discount. But this doesn't mean that it was a logical decision. Instead, it was only supported by logic. If you didn't like the coat, you wouldn't have bought it, regardless of any discount.

Of course, this is only one of the many examples of emotional decisions. I already mentioned marriage as another one. At the end of the day, it's still a decision that you make based on your feelings.

If you focused on logic and statistics, you'd be much less likely to get married. You know that the chance of a marriage falling apart is larger than 50%. And yet, you still do it.

Why?

Because of the emotion that we know as the biggest buy-in – love.

Let's talk about that for a moment.

You have this abstract, gaseous thing that has such a massive impact on your decisions. At the same time, nobody can teach you how to love. Nobody can force you to do it, either. We've all heard the saying that "you just know when it happens".

So, on one hand, you have logic and reason. And on the other, you have something that you can't even explain precisely enough. But it still trumps logic in the vast majority of cases.

With this in mind, why would you try to sell anything based on logic? Why would you talk about the procedures, tools, and techniques you use?

Sadly, this is exactly what I see so many doctors doing. And if you're among them, I can guarantee that it's one of the main causes you're not selling as much as you could.

People don't care about that fancy new machine you have or how it works. They don't care what happens behind the scenes. They only want to know that you can get them the desired outcome. In other words, they want you to move them from pain to joy.

Someone with back pain won't buy from you because your therapy contains this or that procedure. They'll buy so that they can play with their kids, enjoy sex, and wake up without pain. Simply put, they'll buy positive emotions. And you can't sell emotions by focusing on logic.

You need to approach selling the same way as dating. You don't just approach someone and ask them to go to bed with you. You need to go through multiple stages until this happens. In fact, according to a great book that I recently read, there are 12 stages involved:

1. Eye to body
2. Eye to eye
3. Voice to voice
4. Hand to hand
5. Hand to shoulder
6. Hand to waist
7. Head to head
8. Mouth to mouth
9. Hand to face
10. Hand to body
11. Mouth to body
12. Dim the lights

But wait, why am I giving you dating advice?

It's because selling anything works exactly this way! You wouldn't just skip the first eight steps here and touch someone's face randomly. Well, you also shouldn't offer them anything to buy until you've warmed them up.

You need to keep evoking the right emotions for long enough before someone can agree to what you're offering.

Is this how you're selling right now? What are the emotions that you're playing to?

Do you disregard them completely and just keep selling based on dry facts?

If so, you'll want to change your approach sooner rather than later. The moment you do, you'll see how much you can really sell.

The Importance of Using Scripts

So I went over what you need to do in order to sell. Now, it's time to get into the *how*. But first, let me ask you something:

What are the top five questions that a patient asks when they come into the office? When you're doing the presentation, what are the things that people want to know the most?

When you have these questions, think about why patients ask them in the first place. I can give you the answer right now:

It's because you're not addressing them within the presentation.

And this is why following the script is so important. There has to be a clear structure that you should follow to help every patient arrive at the buying decision.

While you're doing so, what's the worst thing that can happen? In other words, what's the worst answer that you can get when trying to sell.

Is it "no"?

This is what most people think. But in reality, it's not the worst answer. Rather, something that you never want to hear is "maybe".

The thing is, both "yes" and "no" are perfectly fine. If someone doesn't want to work with you, they're not the right fit anyway. You only want to focus on those who will agree.

What you don't want to hear is something like, "*Let me talk to my husband/wife.*"

This will only waste a whole bunch of time. There has to be a clear outcome at the end of each sales presentation. And scripts help you tip the scales in your favor and close the deal.

So how do they work?

The best way to explain this is by going through the actual script so that you can see how it works in action. And the script that I'm about to show you can make you *a lot* of money if you stick to it.

The Big Money Close

What are the most important things that your patients want to know before they decide to buy? What are the common objections that you'll have to overcome? How should you structure your presentation?

The Big Money Close answers these, along with many other questions. It's a clear, simple way to maximize your conversions without any struggle.

So how does it work?

When the patient arrives, the first thing that you need to do is give them an overview of who you are and what you do. At this point, you're just reminding them of the things they already know. They've seen your ads and content, so they know what you can do for them. So, in the overview, you're just briefly reinforcing this. It shouldn't take you more than a minute or two to do it. Anything above this will only result in a waste of time.

Next, I already explained that you need to have a clear outcome of the appointment. You want the patient to give you either a "yes" or a "no".

And the way to make this happen is simple – just tell them that this is what you expect. You'll say something like:

"I'm going to walk you through everything. I'm going to go over the procedure, I'm going to walk through the pricing. And in the end, all I ask is that you give me a "yes" or "no". The reason why I ask is that we are not a high-pressure sales place. And if you've made it this far, we find out that most people are ready to move forward. So I'm going to walk you through everything, and can you give me a "yes" or "no" at the end?"

In the vast majority of cases, the patient will agree. And this is where you'll move into the explanation of how everything works.

In our case, back when we were an ED clinic, it would go something like this:

First, we'd tell the patient that they'll receive a custom dose tailored specifically to them. So, if they had a twin brother sitting right next to them, the dose would still be different. We'd tell the patient that we'll order five medications for them, create that unique dose, and then show them how to use it.

This is when we'd get our first objection. People were afraid that they wouldn't know how to inject themselves. They'd have to use the diabetic injection to do it, and this naturally scared some patients.

To proactively deal with the objection, we'd show them how to use it right away. We had a prosthetic penis that we'd use to demonstrate how the patient should use the injection. We'd already fill it with everything they needed, so they'd only have to press the button, and that was it.

Then, we'd tell the patient to stand up, walk around a bit, and they'd get an erection within 10 minutes.

Whatever your treatment or procedure, you need to explain it like this. You don't want to use any big, fancy words, as they'll only confuse the patient. Plus, I already explained that the patient doesn't care about this. So, explain everything as if you were talking to a fourth-grader. Tell them exactly what will happen and what they can expect during the procedure.

During this stage, you should also answer a very common question that patients have:

"Is this safe?"

Again, we did this before the patient even had a chance to ask the question. We wanted to make sure they understand how safe it was from the get-go. So, we'd explain that all medications are made under extremely rigorous conditions and supervision. We'd talk about how this happens to put their mind at ease straight away.

At this point, you're likely to face several objections. And the first one is, *"How come my doctor doesn't know about this?"*

And this is where the importance of standing for something truly shines. I already talked about how you must know exactly what your clinic does and have a signature system. The worst thing you can do is talk about how you do all kinds of things. Instead, you have your system, and that's the only thing you do day in and day out.

With this in mind, the way you handle this objection will look something like:

"I'm sure your doctor is outstanding. But every doctor has a specialty. If you needed heart surgery, would you like a cardiologist that only does that every single day? Or would you want someone who isn't a specialized surgeon but would like to try?"

The answer will be obvious, after which you'll say that you only do that one thing in your offer. We'd say that the only thing our clinic does every day is give people erections. We'd let the patient know that we're absolute experts at that single thing. And you need to do the same.

So what happens after?

Well, this is likely when you might face some doubts from the patient. This is the stage at which you might hear that annoying "maybe".

If it happens, just remind the patient of what you asked them to do – give you a straight answer. And then, encourage them to give you one.

At this stage, you'll get to the vital question:

"How do I pay for this?"

I never let the patient ask this question, and neither should you. After they tell you that they want to move forward, you immediately talk about the payment options. Here's how I used to do it in the ED clinic:

"The cost of the procedure is $5,995. We take the following methods of payment – Visa, MasterCard, Amex, Discover, cash, or cheque. In order to reserve your spot, we require a 50% deposit and final payment 48 hours prior to the procedure. The reason why we do that is that we have to order supplies specifically for you."

This is the overall structure, which you'll adapt to your payment methods. But it's important to ask for something upfront and make sure that there's enough wiggle room. Someone might only be able to put 25% upfront. In this case, ask them if they'll be able to meet the other payments in due time and if they'll proceed if you allow them to give you only 25%.

Another thing that I loved doing was to give people a discount if they pay for everything upfront. I'd give them $500 off if they're able to do it.

And finally, some patients might ask you for financing options, which you should surely have in place. You need to have separate options for those with good and excellent credit. Because when you ask patients about their credit, these are the two answers you'll likely get.

And when you do, tell them that you can offer 12-month financing through a simple in-office application. You never want to let the patient go and have them fill out the application at home. This will open up too much room for doubt. And that's why you want to do it right there on the spot. Pull out your iPad and ask them if they want to do it right now.

This is where you'll get them to think about the final decision. You'll likely face that awkward silence that will make you want to say something. But this is the last thing you want to do. You'll want to remain completely silent until the patient says something. Silence freaks people out, so it will nudge the decision in the right direction.

So there you have it. This is the script that has made me outstanding amounts of money. And if you follow it without deviations, it can do the same for you.

Working with the Non-Buyers

If you apply everything you've read so far in this book, you should convert at least 50% of your first appointments. But what happens with the other 50%?

It's simple – they said "no", so you should just let them go, right?

Wrong!

Here's what I need you to understand:

If someone declined your offer, it only means that they weren't ready to buy at that moment. It doesn't mean that they don't want to buy at all.

When you know this, you can leverage the power of following up to tap into non-buyers and unlock a wealth of revenue opportunities. If you're making $50,000 or so a month, I can guarantee that you're leaving another $10,000–$12,000 on the table by not following up.

How do I know this?

When the recession hit back in the late 2000s, I had to shut down my real estate company. But I still had to find a way to feed my family and pay the mortgage so that we could keep the house.

To make this happen, I worked with my friends in many different niches and industries. These are longtime friends of mine, and we all started around the same time.

I was able to grow their businesses by up to 30% just by targeting their lists. And I made a lot of money along the way.

I did the same thing with my clinic. A large percentage of our growth happened because we targeted non-buyers the right way.

My point is, this is a tried and tested way to add lots of revenue to your practice.

So how do you do it exactly?

Let me use another metaphor that might seem a bit crazy – Chinese water torture. By definition, it's a "painful process in which cold water is slowly dripped onto the scalp, forehead or face for a prolonged period of time, allegedly making the restraint victim insane".

And this is exactly how your follow-ups should work. You'll want to drip your contacts constantly to keep reminding them of you.

Now, you'll want to have a separate campaign for buyers and non-buyers. And you're going to target the latter with different forms of content through a never-ending campaign.

I've been gathering names since 2014. And I think the longest it took for someone to work with me after saying "no" was five years. At some point, they just decided that it was the direction in which they wanted to go.

And this is why you must be persistent. Someone might not agree to work with you for months. But that doesn't mean that you should stop nurturing your relationship with them. You need to keep the campaign going and email them pretty much every day.

I get that this seems like a ton of dreadful work. But it's really not. You can get someone on Fiverr to write all the content and manage your campaigns for you.

And no, sending emails every day won't drive people away. If they have an interest in the topics you're covering, they'll want to keep reading. I can confirm this after 25 years of being a direct marketer and working in 30 different niches. The reason why marketers email people every single day is because it simply works.

So what should the emails be about?

Remember the content calendar that I talked about? Well, this is where you'll want to leverage it. You'll want to focus on creating engaging human content that people will enjoy.

Now, there's no doubt that email campaigns are among the most effective follow-up methods. But they're far from the only one. What I've found that works like a charm is monthly print newsletters. I did it with my real estate company, ED clinic, and many other ventures.

When you have someone's physical address, you can send them these newsletters every month. It's a fantastic way to keep engaging and educating your non-buyers until they eventually change their mind.

On top of this, you can also send postcards, discount coupons, and all sorts of other things. When you do, make sure to follow up again to see if your contacts received them.

You should have these online and offline marketing methods work in concert. While having one way of following up is better than not having any, you'll want to establish as many touchpoints with your non-buyers as possible.

But to do this, you need data. You need people's emails, phone numbers, and physical addresses. The more data you have, the more powerful your campaigns will be. And the more campaigns you run, the more equity you'll keep building for the time you need a cash infusion.

For example, many of my clients saw a drop in their business of around 20% during the COVID pandemic. But when they reopened, they did so with a massive boom because they kept developing and nurturing relationships through content.

And if you do it right, you can have the same results. As a rule of thumb, for every 3,000 names on a list that you regularly contact, there's $1 million in untapped income.

Of course, your list might not be this big right now. You might have a couple hundred people on it. But this is still enough to make a huge difference if you keep nurturing the list. Plus, it will only keep growing. Your list will scale slowly and keep opening up new opportunities to create extra revenue.

So again, just because someone said “no” during the appointment means that this “no” will last forever. If you keep dripping on your list, you can maximize its potential and bring in lots of additional revenue.

You can also use this list as a safety net. If you have to buy new equipment, turn to the list before you seek external financing. In many cases, you’ll see that you don’t even need any. Your list will give you the money you need if you’re consistent with your follow-ups.

So, don’t let a non-buyer get cold and forget about you forever. Grow your list, keep reaching out, and you’ll see how many of those no’s will turn into yes’s.

Maximize Your Conversions

After reading this chapter, think about how different these processes are from what you're currently doing. When you do, you'll likely see that there's a lot of room for growth here.

If you're not sure where to start, take a look at your content. See if it can truly trigger the right emotions and encourage buying decisions. Remember that facts and stats don't sell unless you use them to evoke an emotional reaction.

So don't make your content dry and disengaging. Remember that you're talking to real people with real pain. Address that pain, and then keep showing what you can do about it.

If you do this successfully, you should see more patients showing up for an appointment. And when they do, follow the Big Money Close script to convert as many of them as you can.

If people decide not to work with you on the spot, don't try to force them into anything. Let them go for the moment, and then start following up. You never know if someone will change their mind after a day, month, or a year. But in many cases, they *will* change their mind and decide to go back to you. So, don't miss an opportunity to convert a previous non-buyer.

You now know how to attract and convert more patients. But of course, it doesn't stop there, as it's only one part of the equation. In the next chapter, I'll show you how to give your profits a massive boost with the patients you already have.

CHAPTER 7

Generating Monthly Recurring Revenue

How would you feel if you could add $168,000 per year in pure profit without a single new patient? Well, this is exactly what I helped a client do over the course of five months or so.

The client ran two anti-aging clinics that offered the latest and greatest procedures. However, they were too dependent on these procedures to make money. Worse yet, there was a lot of seasonality in their performance.

The reason for this was their location. Now, I can't tell you the location because of confidentiality. But I can tell you that it was in one of the swing states. These are the states that are highly volatile during political campaigns, when they keep switching from one side to the other. So much money gets thrown into the campaigns that can have a massive impact on pretty much every business.

I know this because we used to deal with it in North Carolina all the time. And I can tell you that it can be quite a challenge. When you pair this with the short shelf life of the practice's offer, you can see why they struggled so much.

Now, our first job was to identify the root cause of all their troubles. And after having a closer look, the underlying issue was glaringly obvious.

You see, the clinic had what I call the open system. Basically, it means that a patient comes in, gets the treatment, and then just moves on. In most cases, they never come back for more.

So why is this such an issue? Why would it bother you if you knew that you could keep getting new people in?

Well, the issue is that you become way too dependent on those one-off sales. You always face that uncertainty of whether someone will come for the procedure. Simply put, there's no predictability or sustainability here.

If you really want to be profitable, you must create a closed system. What this means is that when a patient comes, you want to give them a reason to stick around. And you'll do this through a membership or some form of recurring program.

After understanding how important a closed system is, our client started working towards it. Our goal was to help them ensure that two-thirds of their revenue comes from memberships.

To make this happen, we created two membership tiers – the executive level and the general public level. We structured it in such a way that every offer led to a certain membership. This way, we could close the system and keep more people in.

This model does wonders for practices with a lot of seasonality. Just imagine if two-thirds of all your revenue came in the form of constant and consistent income. Credit cards get charged every month, and life is good. You don't have to wonder when the next big payday will be or where it will come from. Instead, you can rely on the same stream of cash every month, which only keeps growing.

This is what our client got when we developed those memberships. But that wasn't all. We didn't just want the revenue to be stable. We also wanted it to be as abundant as possible. This is why we increased the prices for existing members to be at or above market.

I bet I can guess what you're thinking:

"But didn't this drive existing customers away?"

It's the exact concern that our client had. They thought that raising the prices would make tons of patients go away. But I assured them that less than 5% would. And I was right, as only 1% of all existing patients ended up going away.

This is what happens when you increase your prices the right way and ensure that patients still receive tons of value. There was little to no pushback when we did so, and the client saw how valuable their procedures actually were.

We raised the prices 28% across the board, so it was by no means a small increase. And yet, almost no patient had any objections.

As a result of all our efforts, the client saw a $168,000 increase in annual profit. And all that money came without a single new lead or patient. It was possible purely because we tapped into the clinic's full potential.

Plus, the owner transitioned into only working with executive clients. These clients made up around 7.5% of the entire patient base. But at the same time, they were bringing in about 65% of the clinic's entire revenue.

We made all of this happen in just five months. And we're still far from done. Right now, we plan to increase the prices even further in the foreseeable future. We also have another initiative that should start bringing in another $150,000 or so in pure profit every year.

This is the power of membership models. When you add this kind of recurring revenue to your practice, you can see your profits skyrocket. And more importantly, that money is there to stay. It will keep coming every month, and it can only go uphill if you know what you're doing.

So, if you're still in that transaction-based system, I want you to let go of it as soon as possible. Having at least a quarter of your revenue coming from memberships is better than relying solely on one-off deals. And when you see the perks of recurring revenue, you'll want to keep growing its share in your total revenue.

But how do you make all of this happen? Let me show you what it takes to generate stable monthly recurring revenue.

It's Time to Accelerate Your Revenue

I believe that every business should have monthly recurring revenue. You might already have an idea of why this is true based on my client's story. But the benefits will be even clearer as you move through this chapter.

I've had monthly recurring revenue in every single business I ran. I think it makes everything so much smoother and less stressful. So let me dive deep into this topic, and you'll see why this is true.

What Is Monthly Recurring Revenue?

The concept of monthly recurring revenue is pretty self-explanatory. It's basically the money that keeps coming to your business each and every month. Patients give you their credit cards that go into your system. And every month the money gets transferred to your account automatically.

Now, there are two ways this can happen. You can have all payments coming in on the same day. For instance, I used to have all the revenue come on the first of every month. But then, I decided it was better if it happened on the day when the patient signs up.

It just makes things less confusing on everyone's part. Plus, I love seeing money coming in every single day.

But this is largely a matter of preference. It doesn't really matter how you set it up as long as you do it in the first place. So, let me show you the main reason why you should.

Why Do You Want a Monthly Recurring Revenue Model?

Back in the day, I used to run private clubs, semi-private clubs, and resorts. And I leveraged the membership model to the fullest.

Why?

Because I saw that this recurring income could cover every penny of my operating costs. All fixed expenses, payroll, utilities, and other costs would get covered without any issues. And that's what I want for your practice.

On average, it might cost you $30,000–$40,000 a month to run the practice. So why not make sure that your revenue can always cover them, even if you don't get any new patients. Trust me, this would release a ton of pressure that you might be feeling right now.

Of course, this also includes you getting paid. You don't have to hope that new patients will come in so that you can pay yourself. Instead, you always know how much money you can count on, and everything else is a bonus.

Building Benefits into the Membership

To create monthly recurring revenue, you need to have your beachhead in place. Some people decide to base their core offer on monthly recurring revenue, but I don't recommend this. It can take around six months for you to become profitable with this model, so you need a lot of financial bandwidth to sustain this.

A much better idea is to have your core offer sending people into memberships. And then, you want to pack the memberships with value through all sorts of benefits. You can offer discounts on new procedures or supplements. You can add some exclusive offers available only to members. No matter what you do, the membership needs to have lots of benefits that patients will want to take advantage of.

If you make this happen, members will become your most loyal patients. And this means that they'll be the first ones to try any new methods or procedures that you have. You can basically test their financial viability on your members to see if you should keep moving forward with them. As your members will trust you, they'll be more than willing to take chances that others might not.

The Traps You Need to Avoid

There are many pitfalls of the membership model that you need to steer clear of. And one of the most dangerous is believing that people won't be willing to pay a monthly fee for what you have to offer.

What makes this harder is that such comments might sometimes come from your own staff. They might tell you that they wouldn't agree to the monthly fee that you ask from patients. Naturally, this might make you doubt your offer.

But guess what?

It doesn't matter if your staff wouldn't pay that monthly fee. They're not your prospect!

Besides, membership systems have much less to do with usage than most people think. As I mentioned, I ran multiple private clubs, and I'm still a member of some.

Can I just pay whenever I feel like golfing? Of course! In fact, it would cost me much less to do so. But then I wouldn't have that familiarity and feel-good factors that being a member of a club carries. I wouldn't be able to just walk in and know everyone, have the staff know me, and hang around with those that I enjoy spending time with.

Similarly, I'm a member of a health club just down the street. My whole family is a part of that club. And we only visit it a few times a month. So, for the most part, we're not really taking full advantage of that membership. But we still keep paying for it every month.

My point is, it really doesn't matter that much if people will really use everything that your membership offers. According to statistics, the usage rate for most people in health clubs is only 12%!

This means that for 88% of people, it doesn't make much financial sense to join a club. And yet, they do it anyway!

Think about all the things that you pay every month but don't really use. I bet you can name at least a few of them. It may be a subscription or a service that you don't have that much use for. But every month, you let the service charge your card.

So don't make the mistake of thinking that people won't pay for your membership just because they won't use everything that it offers. If you structure it well, people will gladly sign up and stick around.

Creating the Emotional Bond

Talking about monthly recurring revenue makes it seem like it's all about dollars and cents. But this really isn't the case.

If this is how you and your staff see it, you likely won't get as far as you hope.

Why?

Remember what I told you was the driving force behind every buying decision?

That's right – emotion. I've already explained that you need to make people feel a certain way if you want them to buy from you. And I talked about it in the context of one-off sales. So, imagine the kind of bond that you have to create if you want people to keep giving you their money each and every month.

I can't stress the importance of building and nurturing relationships enough when it comes to monthly recurring revenue. The patient must feel like it makes all the sense in the world for them to sign up and stay loyal to you.

If you want to make this happen, you must get everyone in your clinic on board with the membership. Because it's not just about the relationship between yourself and your prospects. You need to keep strengthening the relationships between you and your staff. And staff members need to know how to maintain emotional bonds with patients.

So, how will you know that you have such a bond?

Well, a telltale sign is when patients start bringing you little gifts as tokens of appreciation. It doesn't need to be anything huge, just something that makes you feel like they're thinking about you.

It can even be a joke. For instance, one of my clients from Wisconsin started focusing on relationships with patients. Some of them would bring him bratwurst all the time, and he's a vegetarian!

It's this kind of bond that will ultimately let you scale your membership. Nobody should feel like they're a part of a transaction where money keeps moving and gets exchanged for services and benefits. Create real, human connections, and your membership can be outstandingly successful.

The Core Messaging Pillars

So we've established that you need to create a strong emotional bond with your patients. The question is, how do you do it?

And the answer is simple – by following what I call the core messaging pillars. Because it all comes down to your messaging. This is how you communicate with a patient in a way that makes them emotionally attached to you.

Let me show you exactly what you need to do.

Before a patient starts working with you, they have all kinds of negative emotions caused by their condition. They might be in pain and feel sad, frustrated, tired, and so on. This is their starting position that you want to move them away from.

And the way you'll do it is through your offer. Once a patient joins your membership, you'll take them from this negative state into a more positive and joyful one. You'll help them get rid of pain and enjoy their life. And you'll keep making their life better for as long as they stick around.

This is what the patient needs to see in your message. But perhaps the best way to explain it is through an example.

Let's say that your offer was HRT. You know how your patient feels because their hormone levels are off. They have little energy, they can't focus, and they're facing lots of challenges on a daily basis.

Now, let's assume that you offer a membership that you name, say, a Master's Program. The membership can give the patient all they need to get rid of all these issues.

The goal of your messaging is to show the patient how they can transition to a happier and healthier state through your HRT program. You need to acknowledge how they feel and say that your program can make all of that go away.

This triggers a strong emotional reaction that will encourage someone to sign up. And when they do and start seeing results, you'll get them into that closed system. They'll see that you can truly deliver on this promise and keep getting the outcome that they need.

Start with Current Patients

So you now have an idea of how memberships work and why you should create them. And here comes the million-dollar question:

How do you sell them?

As with everything else in my framework, there's a clear way to go about it. And it all starts with your current patients. These are the people that you should target with your membership before moving onto a broader audience.

You need to have a campaign that you'll aim specifically at your existing patients. The goal of the campaign is to identify their biggest pain that your offer will solve. Once you do, you'll send out an offer to your current patient base.

You can go about this in many different ways. You can message, send emails, reach out to patients on social media, and even send them postcards, which work really well here.

And then, you're going to bring patients to the clinic and put them into a plan. That plan will be anywhere from $99 to $1,000 per month, which is how much I've seen some memberships are selling for.

So, as you can see, the whole process is very simple. And once you start selling to your existing patients, they'll become your core group that will serve as your financial foundation. They'll be the ones willing to spend their money with you without any objections, which enables you to sleep better.

This should make up for at least 25% of your revenue. This is especially true at the beginning, while you're still setting everything up. And as you go about growing the membership, it should account for 50% of your revenue if you do it right.

At this point, you'll even out so much uncertainty and seasonality in your business. You'll have a reliable stream of income that you can count on, no matter what happens.

Less Stress, More Revenue

You saw the difference that monthly recurring revenue made to my client. And if you do it right, it can do the same for you. You can add outstanding amounts of money to your bottom line without even having to look for new patients.

More importantly, you'll know that all those profits are there to stay. You won't have to fear that the money will disappear in case of any external issues. And I can tell you from experience that this is a fantastic feeling. In our ED clinics, we dealt with floods, snowstorms, and all kinds of issues that would generally stop patients from coming in. But this didn't rob us of our success. Monthly recurring revenue gave us stability and peace of mind during all those troubles.

So how can you structure your membership model? What are the benefits that you'll add to it? How will you establish that emotional bond that I told you about?

It's time to answer these questions and get out of the hamster wheel of constantly having to look for new patients. Close the loop, and keep your patients loyal to you.

Paired with everything else you've learned in this book, monthly recurring revenue can truly transform your business. But the best part is, you can supercharge the system even further.

How?

I'll tell you all about it in the following chapter.

CHAPTER 8

BONUS – How to Put the System on Steroids

Every week, clients in my highest-level group talk to me for 45 minutes. And every time, the call starts with them showing me their numbers. This way, I can help them review their progress and suggest the best way to move forwards.

But there was this one client that didn't want to show me his metrics. He had a successful practice generating over $2.5 million per year. However, $2 million came from insurance, meaning that it took forever for my client to get paid.

This left only $500,000 in cash-based services. Needless to say, it was a horrible revenue structure.

But this wasn't even the biggest issue. Instead, what I found to be the most dangerous thing about the client is that he didn't know his numbers. He had no idea where his clients came from or how much they spent on average. In fact, he couldn't even tell me how much he was making per month, week, and day in the cash clinic.

The client wanted to grow to seven figures. And he surely had everything he needed to do it. Well, almost everything.

You see, my client was highly skilled, and his services were great. He also had an amazing client base. You'd think that someone in his position wouldn't have any reason to struggle.

But he did. And the reason was that he couldn't crunch his numbers, nor was he willing to show them to me.

At one point, I told the client that I'd stop talking to him if he doesn't show me the numbers. And at first, he didn't believe me. He thought that I wasn't serious and that I'd just bend to his will.

But this didn't happen.

Why?

Because my business as a coach isn't to think about customer service, especially when it comes to speaking the truth that my clients need to hear. This client was slowing down his own progress, so I was dead serious when I told him that I wouldn't continue the calls with them.

A few weeks go by, and the client comes back. He'd decided to show me his metrics, and what I saw shocked me.

The client was actually *losing* money on the cash side!

Of course, it was my job to see how we could turn this around. And we found two areas that we wanted to focus on.

The first was the closing percentage of first visits. It went from 20% at the beginning to 70% after we put the right processes in place.

The second thing we had to do was figure out how much it took for the client to acquire a patient. And we saw that acquisition costs were $600. I helped the client get the costs down to $350, which alone ensured that he could make much more from each transaction.

The collective result of our efforts was outstanding. Just by giving the client's closure rate a boost, we added $16,750 *per week* in revenue. Pair this with much lower acquisition costs, and you can see that we've made some serious progress.

During the pandemic, the client's profits actually went up! While everyone was losing, he was winning big. He's now able to buy more patients than his competitors and dominate his niche.

This is what you can do when you understand your numbers. If you asked me what separated winning doctors from those who keep struggling, this would be my answer. You need a deep understanding of your practice's numbers if you want to identify the biggest areas of improvement.

In our clinics, we have a saying:

"The math always wins."

And this is absolutely true!

In this chapter, I'll tell you about the key numbers that you must track if you want to grow your practice. So, let's dive in.

Why You Must Track the Leads Coming into Your Practice

Tracking is critical to your success. Not having any idea of where patients come from prevents you from creating a sustainable and predictable business. If all you do is wing it, you'll waste a ton of money on marketing efforts that don't yield great results. Plus, you'll fail to double down on what works.

Generally speaking, you need to track:

- Where leads come from
- Who books
- Who buys

On top of this, you want to pay close attention to your marketing spend and track your return on investment (ROI). Ideally, you should see a 2:1 or even 3:1 return on your investments if you market wisely.

Now, before I get into this, it's worth mentioning that it's not an exact science. But it's still better than having no science at all and following the strategy of hope. So even though you might not be able to get every single piece of data that I'll talk about, you should be able to get around 80%. And this will be enough to ensure that you can make smart decisions.

To show you why this is true, let me use a metaphor that will perfectly explain how tracking works.

The Bloodwork Example

As a doctor, you rely on science and numbers to help your patients. You base all your decisions on certain metrics that tell you about the patient's overall health.

So let's say a patient comes in, and their bloodwork is horrible. You see tons of signs of heart disease, even though the patient seems healthy at first glance. They're in their 40s, and they tell you that they eat right and exercise regularly.

And yet, their bloodwork indicates that something's off.

In this case, you'd want to dig deeper to find the root cause of their issues. You might order more tests and look at other metrics more closely. Ultimately, you'd go over the numbers until you can see exactly what doesn't work.

And then, you'd use this data to suggest the right course of action. You might prescribe medications or treatments, or tell the patient that they must undergo a certain procedure.

You couldn't make any of these decisions without the numbers. You could, but it would almost definitely be a bad decision.

Well, your business works the exact same way. There's a clear scientific component to it, and you must understand it if you want to grow.

But why?

What is it exactly that you gain once you start tracking your numbers?

Let me show you one of the most important things.

Figuring Out the Rhythm

There are many different metrics that you must track if you want to scale your practice to great heights. And I'll tell you all about them in a bit. But for now, it's crucial to understand that you need to track certain numbers every single day.

I get that this might seem daunting or tedious. But believe me when I say that it's not. You'll have someone in your clinic crunch the numbers, and it will take you 30 seconds to see everything that you need to know.

With time, you'll start noticing certain patterns. And understanding these patterns is vital to maximizing your practice's performance.

For example, in my clinics, I saw that the number of appointments we book on Monday dictated how the rest of the week would go. We realized that we needed to have 25 appointments on Monday to keep seeing good results for the rest of the week. And we also knew that most of those appointments would happen at a later part of the day.

So, for us, this was a hugely important number that we needed to track. Yours will probably be different, so you must figure out which numbers matter to your clinic the most. In other words, you need to understand the following:

The Key Performance Indicators You Need

Do you have all the necessary KPIs in place? If not, you'll want to set them up as soon as possible. Why?

Because doing so lets you see how your clinic is doing in no time. You can be vacationing in Barcelona and take a look at a few numbers, and you'll know everything you have to. You won't need to look at anything else to see if your practice is on the right track.

Now, every business has a specific set of KPIs. But I've found that clinics have a few that they absolutely must track every month, week, or day.

Firstly, I already mentioned that you should book 70% of your first-time inquiries into appointments. Then, you'll measure the show rate, and you'll want to see at least 70% of booked patients actually showing up. And finally, you'll want to convert at least 50% of those appointments into your offer.

So, if someone leaves after that first visit, you don't count them towards the conversion. You also don't do it if they convert the day after, as this falls under follow-up conversions. You only track those who sign up on the spot after coming to their first appointment.

Now, this goes for every practice, no matter what you're selling. Even if you have a $10,000 offer, you should still be able to convert this 50% easily.

The next KPI that you must track is the average revenue per transaction. When you have this number, you can see how much you can pay to acquire a patient.

For instance, if your average revenue per transaction is $1,000, you can comfortably pay $100 to acquire each patient. You might even be able to pay $150 or $200, as there are other factors to consider here. Similarly, if your average is $5,000, then $500 per acquisition isn't a lot, as the margin is still there.

Another thing that you must know is the lifetime value of a patient. There are three ways to grow a practice, and one is to sell more to existing patients.

If you know your patients' lifetime value, you can see what you should do to increase it and get the most out of every patient.

Finally, you must absolutely know your marketing ROI. Marketing is easily one of your biggest expenses, so you must make sure to get as much as you can from every single dollar that you invest.

What this means in practice depends mostly on the industry. There are some industries where I've achieved a 5:1 ROI. In real estate, I even saw a 9:1 ROI. However, these ratios are a bit extreme, so they're quite unrealistic for clinics. In your practice, you're looking for an ROI of 3:1 or so.

So these are some of the main KPIs that you must track. But how do you do it?

The Tools That You Need

If you want to see where your patients come from, you need to leverage the right tools. What you surely *don't* want to do is ask the patient this and take their word for it.

It's not that a patient will lie to you. The real issue is that they might not have any idea of where they've first seen your ad. They might tell you that they've read an article, but they won't tell you which one. A patient might say that they heard about you on the radio when they actually saw your ad on TV.

My point is, you need to have a failproof way of knowing exactly where every lead comes from. Otherwise, you'll have no idea where you should focus your marketing efforts. And this will result in a ton of wasted time and money.

I already mentioned that we used to track every single source of leads very carefully. And doing so gave us a wealth of data that we used to scale the practice to great heights.

For example, we had a leads source called Old School. This was an urban radio station, so around 80%–85% of the audience were African Americans. It was also a very broad demographic, as it encompassed everyone aged 18–65.

A great thing about advertising on Old School was that it was very cheap. It cost us around $25 for a placement. So, we ran a whole bunch of ads around 10–12 times a day.

We advertised on the local talk radio station. The cost of these ads was around $140 per ad, significantly more than Old School.

What we found was that an average Old School listener would call much more than the talk radio listener. They would call two, three, and sometimes even four times as much as talk radio listeners. They'd also spend more time on the phone. However, they wouldn't buy nearly as much.

So, while it was four times more expensive to advertise on the talk radio, we actually made most of our money from it. We realized that just because Old School was cheaper, it wasn't necessarily worth the effort.

This is the kind of data that you can see when you track your lead sources. You'll know exactly which channel is the most profitable so that you can double down on it and stop wasting your resources on things that don't work.

There are many ways to track your lead sources, depending on the type of campaigns you're running. If you're running online ads, you can set up pixels that will track leads and give you a detailed insight into what happens.

If you're using traditional media, you can set up different phone numbers for them. For instance, you can have different phone numbers for radio, TV, and newspaper ads. For our clinic, these traditional channels worked wonders, so this is exactly what we did. We even had specific numbers for each of the radio stations we advertised on, as we wanted a really deep comparison between them.

Of course, this is far from the only thing that we did. So, let me give you a taste of how we used to track leads in our clinics.

How This Works in Practice

I'd like to show you a few examples of tracking that will give you a better idea of how to do it right. And the first example I'd like to talk about was a complete failure. But I feel like these are highly important, as they teach you a lot about what works and what doesn't.

We had this investor in our North Carolina location who was a huge Rolling Stones fan. And one time, the band came to play in Raleigh. The investor got an idea for us to do some event marketing and see if we could get a lot of leads from it.

We decided to put an ad on the side of a box truck. We also had someone distribute flyers at the concert venue. We set up tracking for these campaigns and were ready to see what happened.

The investor thought that the campaigns would kill it. I wasn't that enthusiastic, but I figured that we could get at least some leads from them.

But we didn't; not a single one!

This is how we learned that event marketing is a very specific form of promotion. But at least we gave it a try.

Now, our other avenues were much more successful.

Take Time Warner Cable as an example. From the campaign we did there, we got 71 appointments and 16 reschedules. Overall, we had 61 of these people show up. And 38 of them ended up being patients. Others had issues with blood pressure, weren't a good fit for the program, or didn't join us for other reasons.

But as you can see, we got what we wanted out of the campaign. The show rate was far beyond the 70% threshold, and we converted more than 50% of those first-time appointments.

Our revenue for that month from this campaign alone was $24,000. And it was far from the only source of patients.

As you can imagine, our website was a much more abundant one. These days, a clinic's website is kind of a catch-all, so it doesn't surprise that we saw fantastic results. In one month, we had 161 people book an appointment, and 110 showed up. We made $77,000 in revenue from those we ended up converting.

Of course, these are all simple examples of how tracking works. You can be a lot more elaborate with it, but the basic principle truly is straightforward.

To show you how simple it is, let me go into one of the main things you'll do when tracking your KPIs.

Entering Your Daily Numbers

You'll likely use an Excel spreadsheet to track your KPIs. It's the simplest way to go about it, and I've always relied on it.

Now, in your spreadsheet, you'll have quite some tabs. But your daily numbers will be among the most important ones. It's pretty self-explanatory – this is the tab where you'll enter the relevant data each and every day you're open.

So what data am I talking about here?

Let's say you're entering your daily numbers for the month of May. For simplicity, let's say that it's May 1st.

What you'll do here is set up dedicated columns for a few key numbers.

The first one is the number of unique inquiries. These are the people who call you for the first time to ask about your services. Let's say you had 10 phone inquiries and booked six of them. In addition, you had eight web inquiries and booked two. So, you had 18 inquiries in total, and you booked eight, meaning a 44% booking rate.

Next, you'll want to enter the number of NPEs (new patient evaluations). You'll base this number on the data from the prior day, as it relates to the number of NPEs scheduled in advance for the day you're tracking data.

So for instance, the day before May 1st, you entered four NPEs. And on the first, all four patients show up. This would mean that your show rate is 100%.

Now, you'll want to put in the number of patients you've converted that day. Bear in mind that this only goes for people who sign up that same day. So, if someone shows up on the 1st but signs up on the 3rd, you'll mark this conversion on the 3rd as a follow-up conversion.

Let's say that on the 1st you only converted one patient and that the total revenue was $6,000. Remember that you'll only put in the amount of money that people actually gave you here. So, if someone only gave you a $500 deposit, this is the amount that you'll put in the revenue section.

Everything else goes into the follow-up sales. So, if someone gave you a down payment in February but they paid the balance on May 1st, you'll put it in as a follow-up sale. Let's assume that you had four of such follow-up sales at a total of $12,500.

Based on this number, you'll calculate your follow-up revenue per transaction, which would be $3,125 in this case.

But why is this number important?

It's simple – if you see that it's too low, you'll know that you have to work on your follow-up system. This is the kind of actionable information that you can get by tracking your numbers.

Let's move a day forward and enter all these numbers. Say that you had eight inquiries and booked seven. You had four web inquiries and booked three. You had three shows, three sales, and the total revenue from them was $3,590. There were no follow-up sales and corresponding revenue.

Just by having this data for only two days, you'd be able to draw certain conclusions. Your average booking rate would be 63%, and you want 70%. Your average show rate is 64%, and you want 70% here as well. You can do the same for all other metrics and see if you're meeting your targets. If not, you'll know exactly what stage of the process you need to work on.

See how simple it is? Just by tracking a few key numbers, you can know everything that goes on in your practice. So, set up a tracking system and then start measuring your results.

The Power Is in the Numbers

As you can see, nothing happens in your clinic without there being cold data to support your decisions. Why would you let yourself ballpark everything and hope for the best without knowing what actually happens?

With a simple tracking framework in place, you can identify the biggest areas of opportunity in your practice. You'll know how effective your processes are, and what you need to do to tweak the system and get better results.

Do you have such a framework in place? If not, I suggest creating one as soon as you can. Only then will you truly understand your practice. And this is a powerful position to be in, as it allows you to start moving towards massive improvements.

CHAPTER 9

Bringing It All Together

If you've come this far in the book, congratulations – you now know what it takes to scale your practice to incredible success. As you've seen in the stories of my clients, the system can transform a practice from its core and make a world of difference.

And yet, nothing that you have to do is particularly taxing or complicated. It all comes down to putting a few key things in place.

Remember that it all starts with your beachhead, hence the name of the concept. It's the foundation on which you'll build this entire framework. So, if you haven't already, take your time to truly understand your market, and craft your message and offer based on this deep knowledge.

This alone is often enough to bring about lots of positive changes. Knowing who you are and who you're here to serve is vital to long-term success. It allows you to position yourself uniquely in your niche and dominate it.

With your beachhead in place, it's time to focus on how you show up in the market. In other words, you need to find a way to excite your audience and build lasting relationships with them.

Your content will do this for you, so make sure that it speaks to the right people in the way they want you to speak to them. Understand their pain and what a positive outcome means for them. And then, use your content to show that you can take them there.

While doing so, never talk about the machine or how good you are because of your credentials. As I've said many times in this book, people couldn't care less! They just want to know that you can get them the results that they so desperately need.

If you do all of the above right, conversions will happen much more effortlessly. But you'll still have to land that final punch and make sure you hit that 50% conversion threshold. To do this, follow the script that I gave you, and remember all the principles of conversion that I discussed.

Always leverage emotions, and understand how people think when buying. Evoke the right feelings, and you'll convert without feeling like a used car salesman.

And once you convert the patient, don't let them move on after one procedure. Get them into your membership and start generating monthly recurring revenue. You already saw how beneficial it is, so you know that it's more than worth the effort. After all, who doesn't want an abundant and reliable stream of profits coming in every month?

And finally, don't forget the importance of tracking the results of all these processes. I get that it might seem a bit foreign at first glance. But once you get into the habit of tracking your KPIs, you'll see that doing so is a matter of literally seconds each day.

Whenever you see any red flags in your KPIs, you'll know that it's time to act. You won't waste any time, as you'll know exactly where the problem is occurring. As a result, you'll fix it quickly and efficiently. You'll keep tweaking the system until your entire practice runs like a well-oiled machine.

Remember that successful doctor from the opening of this book? This is who you can become if you follow everything you've learned here. You can have a practice that keeps growing month after month without your involvement growing with it. So much of your success will happen on its own once the system is up and running.

The end result will be more money, freedom, and fulfillment. You'll get to enjoy your life as your clinic keeps scaling. All in all, you'll have the exact life you've been dreaming of.